Welcome to the Scene

An Introduction to the Volkswagen lifestyle

By Brian Moyer

Contents

Introduction to the "Scene"	4
The Basics	13
Car Shows	27
Volkswagen History	40
Acquiring a Car	63
The Daily Driver	86
Project & Show Cars	99
Scarcity & Respecting Rare Cars	108
The Internet	116
Future of the Scene	128

For Rachel,

for listening, encouraging,
and supporting me always...

and

for Mom and Dad,

for raising me to believe
that anything is possible.

Introduction to the "Scene"

I remember the car that ignited my lifelong enthusiasm for Volkswagens. I was 14 and the car was a yellow 1973 Karmann Ghia. It was yellow with a black interior and black Empi wheels. It was lowered and had a dual-carbureted engine and a stinger exhaust. I was hooked from the first moment I saw it. At a young age, I knew I had a serious interest in older cars. After spending countless hours at my uncle's garage checking out his old hot-rods and reading anything I could get my hands on about American muscle cars, it was all but decided that I would end up being a "muscle car guy". That was until I ran into that modified Karmann Ghia.

The story starts even earlier than that. My dad's first car was a 1969 Volkswagen Type III Squareback. Right after I was born, my dad was stationed in Germany with the Army and my parents had a Volkswagen Beetle. When they moved back to the States, both of my parents bought Volkswagen Rabbits. All of my mom's brothers and sisters had Rabbits, and my grandmother had a Rabbit. I had ridden in multiple VWs before I had even learned how to talk.

Much later, after I decided that Volkswagens were the cars for me, I spent days and nights trying to find out as much as I possibly could. I subscribed to *Hot VWs* and *Performace VW* magazines. I went to every car show I could within 100 miles (sometimes more). I went to VW drag races. I helped friends work on their cars. I combed through every junkyard I could find across eastern Pennsylvania. I bought a small mechanic's toolkit. I worked as a lifeguard for three summers and worked loading trucks in the evenings during the school year to save enough money to buy a car and pay for my car insurance. All this pent-up Volkswagen obsession for years, and you know what my first car was? A 1976 AMC Gremlin.

Most of my friends and family were quick to respond with something like "A Gremlin?!? Who on Earth would want to buy one of those? It looks like a giant brown roller skate!" The real reason (though I didn't realize it at the time) was that I was young and impulsive and didn't have the patience to search harder or wait for the "right" Beetle or Karmann Ghia to come along.

It wasn't until I was 19 that I bought my first Volkswagen. It was a 1980 Volkswagen Scirocco. A previous owner had added a Zender body kit, 15" wheels, dual Dellorto carburetors, a performance exhaust, badgeless grill, shaved door handles, 5-speed transmission, the works. The only problems were: 1) I didn't know how to drive stick, 2) I had no clue how to keep a high-performance carbureted car reliably on the road, 3) the engine knocked, 4) the rear inner fenders were rusty 5) the door poppers didn't work and I couldn't fix them, so getting into the car involved a broom handle to the inner door handle through the hatch, 6) you get the idea...

I was in love with my Scirocco. I cleaned it, drove the hell out of it, took it everywhere, and took hundreds of photos of it. I was in modified-Volkswagen-ownership bliss. That was right up until I got T-boned by a Chevy Impala while pulling out onto my parents' street. It was my fault, and the real reason was (although I didn't realize it at the time) that I wasn't a very experienced driver - I wasn't proficient yet at stick-shift. It didn't help that the engine wasn't reliable. After the wreck, I sold the Scirocco to someone from out-of-state on eBay and considered it a "win" because I got all my money back out of it. It never occurred to me that I could have been killed (!) and that I destroyed a beautiful car that I should have been able to pass on to the next owner in as good of shape (or better) that I got it. By now, you might be wondering "Why is he telling me all this?"

The purpose of this book is to share as much of my experience as possible. This book is designed to be a blueprint that I could have handed to 14 year old me to prevent a lot of the mistakes I made (or that others I know made) along the way. I hope any Volkswagen enthusiast will be able to take something of value away from reading this, but it's primarily directed at newcomers. If you are a brand new or relatively new Volkswagen enthusiast, my goal is to inform and educate you as much as possible so that you can get where you want to go as quickly as possible. Also, I want to arm you with knowledge that will hopefully help to minimize destruction (to your car, your budget or yourself).

The Volkswagen "scene" is full of all types of vehicles with all types of owners who have all types of tastes and priorities. This book is oriented toward Volkswagen owners who view their car as, at a minimum, an expression of themselves. (Not just transportation from point A to point B.) Many people who read this book might view their car as some kind of a hobby. The majority will view their Volkswagen enthusiasm as a lifestyle or at least a huge part of it, and then there are the die-hards for which Volkswagens are their life. (Think some kind of combination of working for Volkswagen; owning a Volkswagen repair business of some kind; Volkswagen tattoos; closets, attics or basements filled to the brim with Volkswagen parts and memorabilia.)

No one group is better than any other, and I'm not here to pass judgment. All too often, people are quick to look down their nose at an enthusiast who doesn't share the same views or opinions as themselves. I want to come right out at the beginning and let you know that I support all Volkswagen enthusiasts with all tastes (as long as they're not hateful or destructive to others). If you're here to read a book damning "kids these days", you came to the wrong place. If you are here to learn how to make a million dollars flipping used Volkswagens, you came to the wrong place. If you are here to replace a trade school education or internship working on Volkswagens by reading a book, you came to the wrong place. (You get the idea.)

Who am I and why am I an authority on this topic? I started out as a "DIYer" and worked on my own cars while attending shows and making friends who drove VWs. Then, I got a job at a foreign car repair shop. After about a year and a half, I went to work at a dealership and have worked in new car dealerships ever since. I first started at a Volkswagen dealership in 2005. I've been a technician, service advisor, and now a service manager. All the while, I've been driving Volkswagens, modifying Volkswagens, attending shows and, most importantly, building relationships and making memories.

Niels Bohr, the Nobel Prize-winning-physicist once said, "An expert is a person who has found out by his own painful experience all the mistakes that one can make in a very narrow field." I fit into that category. Most of this book will be written in a "take it from me" or "here's what to do and what not to do" manner. It should not, however, be your only source of information on the topic. This book should be one source of information you use in conjunction with other advice and directions you get from people you trust, for example a trusted technician, family member, car club, internet forum veteran or network of friends.

Later in the book, I will describe what I feel the current state of the scene is. I'll point out some newer tools (specifically online) that might be helpful for you. Also, I'll highlight some systemic changes that are happening, right now as we speak, and what they may mean for the future of the scene. What will be the effect of young people delaying getting their driver's licenses? What will be the effects of Uber, driverless cars and electric vehicles? What will happen to the scene if people keep being destructive to their cars? What will happen to the scene if people keep being destructive at the shows we love? What will happen to the scene if people keep cutting up and parting out "rare" cars?

If you've made it this far, I want to thank you for not just skipping to the "meat and potatoes" of the book. My main goal is to spread my love for the Volkswagen hobby to anyone that wants to learn. For me, it's been a lifetime love affair and I am lucky to say that I have turned what I love doing into a career, and it's awesome. I hope this book will help you to participate in a hobby that has been one of the most fulfilling parts of my life. I've also been lucky to surround myself with family and friends who love VWs too. I've learned invaluable skills. I get to shape and create things with my hands and feel proud when someone else recognizes my hard work. I get to go to several car shows a year and display my car (the culmination of my hard work), but I also get to create some of my favorite memories with some of the best people. I want you to be able to enjoy your car and the VW community (and maybe become obsessed – it happens a lot) without wrecking your finances, personal relationships or putting yourself in harm's way. With all of that said, thanks again for reading and I hope you enjoy it.

The Basics

The biggest (sometimes hardest to answer) question you should ask yourself is, "What is my plan?" There are a lot of choices you will need to make along the way, but you need to start out with a strong mission. Is your Volkswagen going to be your daily driver? Is it a second car that you drive occasionally and take to shows? Will it be a long-term project that you keep in your garage and fiddle with in your free time? Is it going to be a no-holds-barred show car? You don't need to decide right now, but by the end of the book you should have developed a clear idea of what you plan to do with your VW.

As a result, I've structured the book in this way. The reader who wants to start out lightly modifying their daily driver may not be interested in reading about swapping a VR6 engine into a Mk1 chassis. The reader who wants to pull out all the stops on a show car might read about daily drivers and think, "Been there done that." I've grouped cars into three categories. The first is the daily driver. The second is the second car/occasional show car, and the third group is the purpose-built show car. I want to cover as much of the spectrum as possible while keeping the book at a reasonable length. Also, in approaching it this way, someone who reads the book now who is just getting started with their daily driver, might come back in a year and reread it when they pick up a second car. The person who has been modifying the hell out of their Mk3 might come back and read the daily driver section when they pick up a Passat to get to and from work so they can do an engine swap in the Mk3.

When deciding which car to buy and what you plan to do with it, there are many things to consider. Where are you going to store the car? Do you need to drive it every day to work or school? Do you have any technical skills? Do you have tools? Do you have friends or family members with experience? Do you have enough money?

The first, and most important, question is who is going to work on your car. Most other questions stem from this question. I will split this up into three categories. The first is "I don't have a clue how to work on a car and will need someone else to do it for me." The second is "Someone that's close to me knows how to work on cars and will do all of the work or teach me how to do it." The third category is "I'm confident I can do it all myself or at least most of it but can get a small amount of help with what I don't know." There is no wrong answer to this question and you shouldn't be embarrassed to ask it. The important thing is being honest with yourself about your own situation.

Today, I can tackle almost anything mechanical on my cars with very little help, but I wouldn't even attempt bodywork, paint, window tint or machining parts. This puts me squarely in the third category. My problem, when I started out, was that I didn't know what I didn't know. In order to keep my 1980 Scirocco on the road, I soon realized there were a bunch of things that I had no idea about (like tuning side-draft carburetors). I was in the first category but didn't realize it. Therefore, I had to rely on a bunch of help from others.

For those of you that do not plan (at least initially) to work on your car, the most important thing you can do is find someone you can trust to do the work for you. Reach out to friends, family, car clubs, Yelp, Foursquare, Google Reviews, etc. If you live in a metro area, there will many possibilities here. If you live in a more rural area, you may not have as many options. Some dealerships are better than others. Some independent repair shops are better than others. I am not here to guide you in this decision. The important thing is finding someone you can trust who is "your guy" or "your girl" and will do all or most of the work on your car. This step should happen before you even think about buying a car or having any work done.

There are a lot of questions you can ask a potential dealer or repair shop. "What kind of training and experience do your technicians have?" "Do you keep parts in stock for my vehicle, and if you don't have the part I need, how quickly can you usually get it?" "Do you use original equipment parts, and if not what kind of parts do you use?" "What rates do you charge?" These are just some examples, but the idea is that when, not if, your car needs maintenance or repair, you can *trust* the person working on your car. Another factor in this decision is allowing the same shop to do most or all of your work. From my experience, it is never a good idea to take your car to one place for oil changes, another place for tires, another place for state inspections, another place for repairs. This will create headaches for both you and the shops. There is no way for you and "your guy" or "your girl" to build trust. Will my advice cost slightly more up front? Likely. Will it save you money in the long run and make your life a lot easier? Also likely. You see where I'm going with this. One dealer or shop should be taking care of most or all of the work on your car, and you should be able to build *trust* in the people working on your car.

Next is the reader who has little or no experience working on cars but has someone close to them that does. This person can be your parent, brother, sister, best friend, next door neighbor, aunt, or uncle. Someone you know has mechanical experience. Hopefully, they know a thing or two about Volkswagens. The important thing in this category is determining how committed this person is to helping you. My uncle spent long hours helping me repair the brakes on my Gremlin, and a friend of my dad's spent a few weekends teaching me how to replace a distributor and rebuild a carburetor. I had to lean on them for help, and they were willing, but I was lucky. I didn't start out with any kind of a strategy. What I should have done is allowed my uncle to guide me toward what kind of vehicle to purchase (or not purchase!) and seek out his advice at every corner. Instead, I just showed up one afternoon with my Gremlin and his face sank immediately. Our relationship went from one where he was excited to bring me into the hot-rod community to just being an extra chore for him.

If you have this person in your life, I suggest sitting down with them and laying it out on the table that you are interested in buying a Volkswagen. Let them know that you would like their help in picking one out, their commitment to help you learn how to work on it and, most importantly, thank them for their time! Is there something you can do for them in return? Can you mow their lawn? Wash their car? Do you have some other skill that you could offer in exchange? The important thing is being grateful for their help and their time. I wasn't as grateful as I could have been, and now my uncle has passed away and I will never have another chance to thank him.

Communication is key. As long as you both understand up front what they are offering and what your expectations are, this can be one of the best ways to learn how to work on cars. Tons of "car guys and girls" got into the community this way. For many people, this person in your life will only be able to teach you so much and you still may need to go to technical school. (Particularly if you want to make a career out of it.) For others, this might be a parent who is a professional technician, and if he or she teaches you everything they know, that might be all the learning you need to build your own car or break into the automotive industry. Remember - be grateful! One last piece of advice, I would *still* develop a relationship with a dealer or shop of some kind. Unless this person is a professional VW technician, you will eventually need someone else's help, and it's never too early to start this relationship.

As for those in the third category, thank you for taking the time to read this book. Thanks for being open-minded enough to listen to someone else's point of view. I'm assuming that you have sufficient confidence in your mechanical abilities to tackle almost anything on your car and you're here for another reason. Maybe you heard this book kicked ass and you wanted to read it. Maybe you're here to hate and flame me online or at a show. (I hope not.) Most likely, you are freshly out of technical school, coming to Volkswagen for the first time from another brand or you've been working repairing cars but want to branch out into the show scene or modifications. My advice to this group is to not be overconfident in your abilities. You only get better if you're constantly learning. You do not know everything (despite what you may think). If you don't already work at a shop, you should still develop a relationship with a dealer or shop for those things that you can't tackle yet. It's OK to ask for help.

The next question is where to store your car. If you plan to do any work yourself, you really need to ask yourself where that will take place. Growing up, my parents never had a garage and most kids I knew were in the same boat. A few kids' parents had a one car garage, but you can imagine what kind of conversation might have been had when asking to use it for a few weeks (or months or years) to take your car apart and replace the engine. (That doesn't cover oil stains on the concrete, other kids hanging out there, or parts and friends' cars littering the driveway outside.) If you are lucky enough to have your own garage or a person helping you will let you use their garage, this is not an issue. When I had the Gremlin, I rented a one car garage for $65/month which was not a small amount of money to the average 17-year-old in 2000. Later, I rented a 30'x30' garage with a close friend. That was the point when the possibilities really opened up. I don't remember the exact cost, but it was something like $75 each per month, which again, was not a small amount of money but totally worth it.

OK, you've decided who will work on your car and where it will be worked on. The next step if you plan to do any of this work yourself is tools. In my opinion, this is an *investment*. It is a necessary expense. Tools don't depreciate much and will always be useful. As long as you have your health, you will always be able to use them and you can always give them to someone else if you decide to give it up or can't do it anymore. Tools help you accomplish something of *value* or keep you from having to exchange your money for someone else's time. If you acquire the knowledge of how to use them, tools are an investment in yourself.

There are three general pitfalls when it comes to tools. The first is buying poor quality tools. Tools need to be of a high enough quality that they will always be reliable. You should be able to give your tools to your kids and them to their kids, and their kids' kids. You get it. The second pitfall is buying way more tools than your skill level requires. If you haven't been to technical school or you don't work as a professional technician or you are a brand new professional technician, you do not need a gold-plated 6' x 8' toolbox bursting with shiny new tools. Unless you are independently wealthy, one way or another you exchange your time for money. Do you really want to tie up $10,000 in shiny tools in a shiny toolbox that you don't know how to use? For that money, you could build a sweet car that you can *enjoy*. As far as I know, there are no toolbox shows where they give out trophies for the fanciest tools. Even if there were, I wouldn't want to be a part of it. I'm getting a little silly here, but the bottom line is: buy only what you need and make sure that what you do buy is of excellent quality.

The third pitfall when buying tools is compound interest. This isn't a personal finance book, so I won't dig into this too deeply, but *the quicker and better you understand compound interest the easier your life will be.* When you borrow money, you are paying someone else to use their money for a given period of time. When someone lends you money, they are earning profit on the money they allow you to borrow. If a 20 year old were to use compound interest to their advantage by investing $1,000 in a 401K or IRA (and never invested another red cent) and it earned an average of 8% a year (a conservative estimate for an S&P 500 index fund), that $1,000 would become over $30,000 by the time that person reached 65 years old. Remember, especially if you're still young, that that 8% (or 12% or 15% or 20% or 25%) interest you are paying in interest on your tools is costing future-you tens of thousands of dollars.

Work on making yourself wealthy, not a money lender. Read all you can and make sure you understand it. If you're going to be involved with money, you want to be on the receiving end of compound interest, not the paying end. Way too often, hobbyists and professional technicians borrow thousands of dollars to spend on tools and toolboxes at double-digit interest rates. This is a great way to donate money to your tool guy's boat, truck, house or kid's college fund, but it won't help you build wealth or become less dependent on others. Buy tools with cash if possible. If you need to borrow money check your bank or credit union for the lowest possible interest rate. Please take a moment or two to understand the effects of compound interest on your life. Moving on.

You've decided what you plan to do with your car, who's going to work on it, where it's going to be worked on and you have a basic idea when it comes to tools. A vision should be starting to gel in your mind. The next step for most people is to pick the right car; this may not be the case for everyone. If a relative just gave you their 1983 Rabbit GTI or you already have a 2002 Jetta Wolfsburg Edition, you might be tempted to skip ahead. Please stick with me. I think you can still get something out of this next bit.

What car you want to drive is completely subjective and slightly different for everyone. Maybe you want the same kind of car as someone you know. Maybe you can't stand the idea of having the same car as people you know. Maybe you saw a Karmann Ghia in a movie and always knew you had to have one. Maybe your first car was the one that got away, a 1987 Cabriolet, and you always wanted to buy another one and fix it up. This is the magical part of the enthusiast community. There is no wrong answer.

If you've accepted that cars don't have to be the same as buses, trains, bicycles, horse-drawn carriages, rickshaws, mopeds or subways (ways of getting from point A to point B), then you've accepted the irrational but acceptable notion that cars can be something more. They can be a source of some of your favorite experiences. They can be a part of some of the greatest memories of your lifetime. They can be an expression of yourself - no different from paintings, sculptures, graffiti, clothes, tattoos or symphonies. Granted, they might not be appreciated that way by everyone, but how many people do you know who get that jazzed about sculptures, either? (I'd like to take this moment to personally apologize to all sculpture-enthusiasts who might be reading this, along with the family and friends of sculpture enthusiasts everywhere.)

Car Shows

One of the most exciting parts of the VW scene for me has always been car shows. This is what all the hard work is about. This is when you get to spend pure unadulterated time looking at cars, talking about cars and spending time with your favorite car people. Some of the very best weekends of my life have been spent walking among rows of impressive VWs, spending time with my wife and friends as well as the associated late nights eating, drinking and partying.

For the uninitiated, car shows are events where cars are typically put into groups and then judged. Trophies or prizes are usually given out at the end. When I'm talking about shows, a lot of what I talk about will apply to get-togethers, cruises and "cars & coffee" type events, but to keep it simple, imagine I'm talking strictly about car shows. Some people attend as spectators and for a lot of people, this is one of several or many hobbies. For some people, the car show scene is a lifestyle. This doesn't make any one person more or less "hardcore" than anyone else; I just wanted to point out that different people get different things out of car shows.

My first car show was a hot-rod show in rural Pennsylvania. If I wasn't completely hooked on modified cars before I went, I was a goner the moment I got there. I remember walking around and looking at the cars, mostly from the '30s, '40s and '50s and being in complete amazement. My jaw must have dragged on the ground behind me all afternoon. What was immediately striking was how different the cars were from stock ones: bright colors, metal-flake paint, flames, scallops, huge chrome engines with short exhaust pipes, huge rear tires, some with fenders, some without fenders, some with engines out of completely different cars, some without door handles. As the afternoon went on, the other thing I started to realize is that the majority of the owners had done some or all of the work themselves. And, as I would later find out, mostly in a one or two car garage at their house.

It never occurred to me until that day that hot-rods didn't just come that way. My thoughts had never been tested but I bet if you had asked me, I would have guessed there was a hot-rod dealership somewhere that you just walked in and bought one and that's it. I began to realize that if all these people had been able to build something so incredible that I would one day be able to build something like that myself. Also, I started to realize that most of the cars were some kind of work in progress. The more and more people you talked to, the more you realized that almost nobody's car was "finished". You also couldn't help but notice the pride they had in their car and the camaraderie there was among the people.

Nowadays, I go to air-cooled and water-cooled VW shows instead of hot-rod or muscle car shows, but the differences mostly end there. Most of the owners do some or most of the work themselves, very few of the cars are ever "finished" and the new ways people keep finding to modify their cars never cease to impress me. Most of all, you notice the pride and camaraderie. After you've been to a handful of shows and start talking to a few people, you'll start to notice a lot of the same faces over and over, and hopefully you're able to build some valuable and lasting friendships.

I'd like to spend a minute talking about cars as artistic expression. I don't think a lot of people look at it this way, but that's the way I see the car show scene. It's not very different from music, writing, painting, making musical instruments, etc. There is a level of craftsmanship involved that I believe is completely under-appreciated. The making of a legit show car to me is no different than making an album or writing a book. It starts with a concept in your mind that you want to physically express. I think this is what, more than anything, attracts people to this hobby. People recognize not only how beautiful and expressive objects can be, but they recognize the effort that went into the making of them. This is the same reason people will spend nearly unlimited amounts of money on a specific Fender guitar, a Banksy piece or a certain Katana.

One of the main reasons I've chosen this lifestyle is wanting to see people constantly pushing the boundaries of what I thought was possible. When I first started going to VW shows, I scoured every car trying to notice every single detail, hoping not to miss anything. Everything was new to me and I felt pulled in a hundred directions. After a while you start to get this feeling that everyone has done everything and you can't be surprised any more, until you are inevitably surprised again. Every year someone finds a new combination that I didn't think was possible. They find new ways to make things simpler, which is to say more beautiful. Sometimes I'm dumbfounded looking under the hood of a car trying to wonder how this elegant, violent thing even moves or stops.

This is why people subscribe to car magazines. This is why people spend seemingly unlimited time on car forums. This is why people go to car shows. This is why people start car clubs. You get a taste of that excellence and you want to become a part of it. My only advice is that over time, you might struggle and lose sight of what's important to you. What's important is wanting to witness the boundaries being pushed and to be a part of it. When it's wintertime and your engine is sitting on the garage floor next to your car and you're struggling to make the effort to go work on it, try to remember why you got into this.

After a while, you might also fall into the everyone has already done everything trap. You'll feel like you've seen every color of Mk2 GTI on every combination of wheels with every combination of engine. Eventually, something new will pop back up. Better yet, I encourage you to create or help a friend create something new to blow everyone else's mind. There are literally infinite opportunities to create "your" car. Even better, after you've created one, you can create more if you like. Even though you'll see tons of cars that all seem to look alike, remember there is always the possibility of something new. Try not to fall into the "let's all be different together" trap. In my mind, it's even better to try to make something completely unique.

The other reason I keep sticking with this hobby is the people. I get so excited about these weekends away from the daily grind that I'll frequently request the time off from work and book a place to stay almost a year in advance. I plan my whole year around things like, "I can't do that, that's SoWo weekend." When I was a teenager in the late '90s and early 2000s, a close friend and I would take every opportunity possible to go see any car show (especially VW show) within a few hours of our hometown. Sometimes, this would involve things like skipping school on a Friday afternoon to drive 90 minutes to Englishtown, NJ to watch people rolling into Waterfest. We were too young and didn't have enough money to stay the night, so we'd watch the cars roll in for a few hours and turn around and drive home. The next morning we'd turn right around come back, spend all day at the show and drive home again that night. Other times, we'd pile our girlfriends in a lowered car and drive two and a half hours to the Beaver Springs dragstrip to watch air-cooleds duke it out all afternoon. We'd both flinch every few minutes the whole way there when the fenders rubbed the tires because so many people were in the car.

Now I'm much older, a father, have a job, live in a different state, have new friends and go to different shows, but if anything, it's even more fun. Personally, I've never built a "show stopper." I've gotten lots of compliments on my cars and a handful of awards, but I've never gone all in on a best-in-show type car. Most of the reason is because I was a young father trying to support a family in a tough economy. Also, I used to feel I was pulled in too many directions and tried to dedicate myself to too many hobbies and never excelled in any one in particular. Over the years I've learned to let some of the distractions fall by the wayside, but I still have a ways to go.

One day, I expect I will build a showstopper, but that's not necessarily the point. That's something you find out after years in this hobby and life in general. At any given time, the people you know might move around, have some money, not have any money, have a project, not have a project, they might be on top of the world or they might be going through some shit. The very best car people are the ones who keep showing up and enjoying time with their friends no matter how life is going at the moment. They may not (and many times won't) have the nicest car (or a car at all), but that's not what it's really about in the end. Sure, there are those handful of people who work hard day in and day out to build the best cars and when that accidentally combines with life going their way for a while, it seems like they can't do any wrong. Life can kick you in the ass at any time. I completely respect the people who put together the nicest cars, but even more, I respect the people that keep showing up year after year regardless of their car because they love being a part of it.

All that said, if you have the patience, money, opportunity and/or the talent, I say go for it. Build the very nicest car you can. Even if it takes a few years (or decades) and you have to go to shows in your beat up non-VW daily. You only live once. Just make sure that you keep things in perspective and don't get down on yourself. Enjoy the time with your family and friends. In the words of Hunter S. Thompson, "Life should not be a journey to the grave with the intention of arriving safely in a pretty and well preserved body, but rather to skid in broadside in a cloud of smoke, thoroughly used up, totally worn out, and loudly proclaiming 'Wow! What a Ride!'"

Different people get different things out of the car scene. People like to ask my why I've had so many cars and why, I can never hold on to them for a very long. For me, personally, it's mostly that I enjoy working on them. I like bringing them back from whatever rough state I find them in (usually not having run in a while). I also enjoy the thrill of the hunt. Once every year or two, I like saving up as much money as I can at the time and going on the hunt for the next big project. Frankly, I also get bored with a car that is too finished. I prefer to spend a few hours working out a drivability bug or making something work better than detailing a nearly perfect car. That's just my specific opinion. Other people prefer to do other things.

One thing I will specifically ask you to do is not focus on status. This is most commonly referred to as trying to earn "scene points". You don't have anything to prove to anyone. Nobody really cares if you went to a show before they shut it down or moved it. Nobody really cares if you know the owner of a certain shop. Nobody really cares that your car is the lowest and breaks stuff all the time. There are lots of "before they were cool" things in the car scene that most of us actually do love: old-school rims, old-school valve covers, rear window louvers, etc.

What we can't stand is the competition for status. This is not a personal attack on anyone in particular, but some examples are: wearing a shirt from seven years ago for the show you're currently at, more than about two degrees of negative camber, flaring your fenders with a pair of pliers or a baseball bat, who's got the most "OG" air freshener, egging people on to do burnouts and recording it, anything involving trying to humiliate a police officer or cop car and recording it, posting mercilessly on social media from the show you're at to prove you were there and how cool you were...you get the idea. Generally, if you're a fun person to be around and/or you have a particularly nice car, people will want to be around you. It's not a competition for status though. This isn't the high school lunchroom. We do like clever or cheeky things like dressing up as a banana or a chicken. We like self-deprecating jokes about your own car. We *do not* like anything that is destructive to other people, their cars or a town hosting the event. Period.

A couple of excellent world-class shows (I'm thinking Waterfest, SoWo, H_2O) have been at times completely ruined by this movement. If you want to stand in a crowd of a hundred people and egg a young woman on to flash you, go to Mardis Gras. (Also, please stop reading this book and don't ever affiliate yourself with this hobby in any way.) If you want to see people drift or do burnouts, go to a racetrack. If you want to see people doing illegal things directly in front of cops, I don't have any sound advice for you - you sound like a psychopath. Kidding aside, this is what is ruining and fragmenting the Volkswagen scene. I am all for getting a little rowdy with your friends, as long as it is respectful to others and doesn't harm others in any way. I don't have a problem with a little legal day-drinking and having a good time, but if it involves DWI or escalates into a near-riot atmosphere, you are embarrassing us all and you're hampering our ability to have a good time with our friends without being kicked out. Also, you're probably in some way risking going to jail. Please, don't be "that guy".

Volkswagen History

Before you select your car, I should hit on a few high points of Volkswagen history and a few vocabulary words that you will want to know. Volkswagen came about when Adolf Hitler commissioned Ferdinand Porsche to make a spartan, low-cost car for the German citizens. This car quickly evolved into the iconic Beetle. I'm not going to go into too much depth, but suffice to say that they sold thousands to German citizens leading up to World War II. After the war, the company was rebranded as Volkswagen, which translates to "people's car", and the company was owned by the West German government. Soon after the war, Volkswagen started to export the Beetle all over the world, and it first arrived in the United States in about 1950.

All Volkswagens in the United States up to 1975 were air-cooled, rear-engined, and rear-wheel-drive. Let's define those three things. An engine is air-cooled if it uses air flowing over itself to keep from getting too hot (as opposed to coolant flowing itself). I can't think of any modern car that is still air-cooled, although some motorcycles and other types of engines still are. This was an excellent design for the time because it kept the total number of parts low, the building cost low, and it withstood the extreme cold in northern Germany.

Rear-engined is what it sounds like: the engine was in the back of the car. If you opened the hood, all you found was a small luggage compartment and a spare tire. Again, very few modern cars have this design (mostly high-performance "super cars" and plug-in electric cars). Rear-wheel-drive means the rear wheels propel the vehicle forward. This is still prevalent in the majority of trucks, vans, some SUVs and larger or higher-performance cars. The majority of modern cars are front-wheel-drive.

In 1975, the Volkswagen Rabbit and the Volkswagen Scirocco came to the

United States. They were water-cooled, front-engined and front-wheel drive. This was a bold move for Volkswagen, being opposite to the design that put them on the map. Why did Volkswagen move to this design and stick with it all the way up to the present? For whatever reason, people had simply stopped buying Beetles. The design at this point was about 25 years old in the U.S. and around 50 years old in Germany. People were ready for something new.

I have equal love for air-cooled cars and 1975-present "water-cooled" cars. I have owned some of each and plan to continue to do so. This book, though, is going to be primarily about water-cooled cars. Why would I cut the brand in half this way? There is already a saturation of information about air-cooled cars available. All you need to do is pick up a copy of the book *How to Keep Your Volkswagen Alive* or check out www.thesamba.com/vw to get plenty of information to get you started on that. I'm not saying an air-cooled enthusiast wouldn't find this book useful (I hope they would), but information on these cars is exhaustive and has been in print for a long time in some cases. Another point it that most air-cooled cars have already been quite collectable for some time, and the price of even a fair condition 1966 Beetle or 1963 Bus will dwarf a fair-condition 1983 Rabbit GTI or even a 2005 GTI. If owning a classic Beetle, Bus, Thing or Karmann-Ghia is your life's dream, don't let me stop you. I have a 1961 Beetle project right now. Go for it! I wish more people were dedicated to preserving them, it's just not largely going to be the topic of this book.

For the straightforwardness and simplicity of this book, I plan to write mostly about "A" and "B" chassis cars. I will also mostly be excluding the Eurovan, Touareg, Routan, and a few others. You can divide the vast majority of modern Volkswagens into two categories. A-chassis cars include Rabbits, Golfs, Jettas, New Beetles, Rabbit Pickups, Jetta Wagons, Golf Rs, Corrados, Sciroccos, etc. B-chassis cars include the Passat, CC, Dasher, Quantum, etc. Generally speaking, the A-chassis cars are smaller than the B-chassis cars and more abundant because Volkswagen made more of them. There are quite a few enthusiasts who have

Passats and CCs and the like, but based on sheer number of cars made, the overwhelming majority of enthusiasts' cars are A-chassis cars.

A-chassis cars can be divided into several different categories or "Marks." When reading this in a book or online, you will see Mk1, Mk2, Mk3, etc. This is an abbreviation for "mark one" or "mark two." Most people also pronounce it this way. Since the advent of internet forums, a large group of people who learned about them almost entirely by reading about them on the internet started to pronounce them "emm kay one" or "emm kay two." This is less correct, but has become acceptable in a lot of circles. Pronounce it however you like - just know that if you choose the latter, some people may try to correct you or you may catch an occasional eye-roll. Again, I'm not here to judge. I'm just happy you're an enthusiast.

Now for a little information on B-chassis cars. Each generation of B car is numbered, so B1, B2 ... B6, up to the current B7 Passat. Right now enthusiasts are driving quite a few B5, B5.5, B6 and an increasing number of B7 Passats. There are still some B3s and

B4s, but increasingly those cars are becoming donor cars (having their engines, transmissions and other parts harvested for use in other cars). The B1 and B2 in the U.S. were the Dasher and Quantum, respectively. There aren't many B1 or B2 cars at your average VW car show, and a clean, well-done one will always turn some heads. Some of the most common cars on the road today are probably the B5 & B5.5 Passats. These were built from 1998 to 2005. They are primarily 1.8L turbo engines or 2.8L V6 engines. A few came with manual transmissions, but the majority came with automatic transmissions. There's also a wagon version, some are AWD and some even have the "W8" eight cylinder engine. A brief Craigslist search in your town will probably turn up one or several of these for sale at all times, so they are relatively easy to get your hands on.

Next after the B5 in popularity (as of this writing) would be the CC, which has been made from 2009 all the way up to present. The vast majority are 2.0L turbo engines mated with a "DSG" transmission. The acronym stands for Direct-Shift-Gearbox. Volkswagen has been using this transmission in some of its vehicles for about ten years now. My current 2014 Mk6 GTI has a DSG and I love it. The CC is a full-sized coupe. They have four doors, four (later models have five) seats, and are relatively luxurious for a Volkswagen while still being a blast to drive.

The B7 Passat in the United States is manufactured in Chattanooga, TN. This is a huge step for Volkswagen, as they didn't manufacture any car in the United States from 1985 – 2011. In 2012, the new Passat was released. It's a brilliant car. They come with a variety of engines and configurations. There are a handful of people heavily modifying these cars already, but this is still mostly uncharted territory. Based on the sheer number of Passats that Volkswagen is selling in the U.S., I believe these will remain very popular with enthusiasts for a very long time.

As for the A-chassis cars, we should start at the beginning with the Mk1. The Volkswagen Mk1 holds a special place in many Volkswagen enthusiasts' hearts. Volkswagen brought the Rabbit and the Scirocco to the U.S. in 1975, just as the price of gasoline was starting to skyrocket. As a result, these fuel-efficient, fun-to-drive cars became an almost instant hit. The Rabbit GTI, specifically, is one of the most iconic cars Volkswagen ever made. It was a high-performance, fuel-injected, front-wheel-drive hatchback at a time when Detroit was making some horrendous low-performance, still-carbureted, rear-wheel-drive sedans.

The Mk1 came in many varieties: two and four door Rabbits, two and four door Jettas, two body styles of the Scirocco, the Cabriolet (German for "convertible") and the Rabbit Pickup. The Fox was also an A1 but is not usually included in the Mk1 discussion because of its longitudinal (front-to-back instead of side-to-side) engine design and having been made in Brazil instead of the U.S. or Germany. Occasionally, someone will build a particularly cool Fox. They also make great daily drivers, but they're sort of in their own category.

Mk1s, like many Volkswagens, had a mostly modular design. Most engines, transmissions, interior parts, windows, trim, brakes, suspension, etc. are interchangeable between years and models. This is one of the most attractive parts of the Mk1 for many people. There are endless ways to make your Mk1 your own. As a general rule of thumb, like with many manufacturers, not just Volkswagen, the two door models are more desirable than the four door models. If you're not looking to build a show car, this might make a four door Rabbit or Jetta more attractive because they can be had for less money, but they aren't the most collectible and for the most part aren't chosen to build serious show cars.

One final thing about the Mk1 before we move on would have to be the CIS injection system. CIS is a mechanical fuel injection system manufactured by Bosch in the 70s and 80s. It works really well for what it was designed and these cars can be quite fuel-efficient and reliable. That said, CIS is not like modern fuel injection - there is no computer to scan for fault codes. If you choose a CIS car, you (or your mechanic) had better go through it thoroughly to make sure everything is operating as it should before even considering using it as a daily driver. Lots of people have their Mk1 dreams dashed temporarily or permanently by malfunctioning CIS that they don't know how to fix. I'm not trying to scare you away - Mk1s are my favorite water-cooled car - I'm just asking you to be aware.

The Mk2 came with many design improvements over the Mk1. There are also fewer variations of the Mk2. They are limited to the two and four door Golf, two door GTI, two and four door Jetta and the Jetta GLI. Although the Cabriolet was still being made at this time, it was a Mk1 all the way through 1993. Mk2s came in gas and diesel variations with automatic and manual transmissions. Most everything is interchangeable between models. Just like the Mk1s, the most collectible models are the two door models. The 1985-1989 cars are "small bumper" cars and 1990-1992 cars are "big bumper" cars. The 1990-1992 GTIs are the crème de la crème of the Mk2. They came with 134 horsepower 2.0L 16 valve engines, close-ratio 5-speed transmissions, bigger brakes, 2-piece BBS RM wheels and Recaro seats. In original, not heavily modified condition, these are some of the most collectible water-cooled Volkswagens out there. In the past few years, there has also been a movement toward collecting or modifying Jetta coupes and Golf GLs. Starting with some 1989 models and all 1990-1992 models, Volkswagen went to "CE2" wiring, which was a wiring system consistent across all of its models. This doesn't make the big bumper cars vastly superior to the small bumper cars, but it does make engine swaps a whole lot easier. The engine electrical harness from all the CE2 cars just plugs right into the fusebox of all other CE2 cars. (The 2.0L ABA, ALH diesel and the VR6 being some of the most popular.)

The Mk2 is a sweet spot for a first enthusiast car. If the Mk2 fits your taste, you really can't go wrong with almost any option. The only thing I would say is that most people would advise to stay away from an automatic transmission. The digifant injection system cars are easier to keep on the road than the early CIS Mk2 cars, but I wouldn't let that deter you from buying a 1985 Golf, for example. My advice regarding how unusual and temperamental CIS can be from the Mk1 section would still apply here. Many people I know started out in a Mk2 Jetta, Golf or GTI and enjoyed them for years. Two of my most recent project cars were a Montana Green 1992 GTI that I swapped an ABA engine into and a 1987 16V GTI. Both were easy and fun to work on and an absolute blast to drive. Again, it all boils down to your own personal taste, but it's hard to go wrong with a Mk2 as an enthusiast's first VW.

I will make a couple brief comments on the Volkswagen Corrado. It was available from 1989-1994 in the US (1995 Canadian models are highly collectible) and had two available engines: the supercharged G60 four cylinder and the VR6 six cylinder. Inside the enthusiast community, they are kind of polarizing. Not quite Mk2, not quite Mk3. You basically love them or hate them. They are some of the best looking and most fun cars to drive, but they can be more difficult to work on than other A2s or A3s. Also, most of them have been driven pretty hard at some point in their life and will need quite a bit of TLC to make them a show car or reliable daily driver. I'm not passing judgment. If you feel like you have to have a Corrado, don't let anyone tell you otherwise. With these cars, maintenance records and the car's history are more important than almost any other VW. If you're buying a G60, receipts for replacement or rebuilding of the charger are essential. You should build into your plan the cost of rebuilding it, if necessary. With the VR6 cars, the same goes for cooling system parts and timing chains. If there is no record of those, you need to build that cost into your budget.

The Mk3 is an even better, perhaps quintessential, first car for a Volkswagen enthusiast. They are abundant, reliable, inexpensive and fun to drive. They came in the form of a two and four door Golf, a four door Jetta, two door GTI and the return of the convertible (this time the Cabrio instead of the Cabriolet). These cars aren't truly collectible yet, but I'd bet that in the future the most collectible ones will be the two door GTI, the VR6 Jetta GLX and the diesel Jetta. There were also several special editions of the Mk3 like the K2, Trek, Wolfsburg Edition and Harlequin. The only seriously collectible one so far has been the Harlequin. If you don't know what it is, take a moment to Google it. Only around 250 were originally made and I would bet someone could fairly easily track almost all of them down. (In other words, the unfortunate likelihood of "finding" one that doesn't already belong to an enthusiast is almost nil.) Also, bonus points go to my wife who, at a glance, can point out a "red" Harlequin or a "yellow" one, whatever the case may be.

If you are looking for an inexpensive but fun daily driver, you've found it in a Mk3. If you are looking for a stout car to swap in an R32 engine or 1.8T, look no further. For the price of most Mk3s, you really can't beat the value. Right now, the only problem with the Mk3 is that they aren't considered classics yet, and a lot of people have moved on from them as daily drivers. For a few thousand dollars, it is really hard to find a nicer car than a VR6 Mk3 GTI, a GLX Mk3 Jetta or a TDI Mk3 Jetta. In my opinion, this is about the most bang for your buck you're going to find right now. They are still relatively "simple" cars like their predecessors. There are very few complicated-to-understand electronic components. I predict an eventual resurgence in Mk3 values, but if you're just getting into the Volkswagen scene right now, you're in luck.

The Mk4 family of cars in the U.S. included a two and four door Golf, a four door Jetta sedan, the first Jetta wagon, the R32, two and four door GTIs, and the Jetta GLI. (The New Beetle is an A4 although no one uses that term to describe it.) The face-lifted Cabrios being sold at this time were as more Mk3 than Mk4 and are commonly referred to as "Mk3.5." The first Volkswagen that I purchased brand new was a 2002 GTI. It was red with a black interior. It had a 1.8T engine and 5-speed manual transmission. To this day, it was one of my favorite cars I've ever owned.

The fourth generation cars saw a giant leap forward in terms of technology. These cars are considerably more complex than their predecessors. A handful of advances were the anti-theft immobilizer, the first turbocharged gasoline engines, body control modules, and those beautiful blue and red gauges. (Also have you ever noticed that most Mk4s smell like crayons inside?) I won't go into much more detail on this, but you can fix almost anything on a Mk3 with a simple mechanic's toolset, whereas the Mk4 is has more electronics. This is not said to deter you - far from it. My wife's car for years was a 2004 Jetta and she loved it. Whether it's a daily driver or an all-out show car, the Mk4 is a great canvas. They're just a little more complex to work on than the earlier cars.

The Mk4 also had several serial-numbered and special edition cars. These were a big deal in their day. There was the 337, the 20th anniversary GTI, the Jetta GLI and the R32. These are far and away the most collectible cars from this era. I could safely be accused of being a Volkswagen "purist". I will touch on this in a later chapter, but I implore you, if you come into possession of a relatively unmolested one of these cars, please leave it in as good of shape or better when you are finished with it. There are plenty of other Jettas, Golfs and GTIs to modify. Please don't do anything to one of these cars that can't be reversed. OK, I'm off my soapbox, but no really, please don't do this. Also, automatic transmissions are fine for daily drivers, but they're not as spirited as the later DSGs. For a weekend car or show car, you'll probably want to find a manual.

The Mk5 platform was a total transformation from the Mk4 platform. The cars were completely overhauled mechanically and stylistically. The Jetta was available from 2006-2010, while the Rabbit and Rabbit GTI (a throwback to the Rabbit name from the Mk1 in the US) were only available from late 2006-2009. There was no Mk5 Jetta Wagon, but there was the Eos, Beetle and Beetle convertible, all based on the Mk5 platform. The Mk5 brought the 2.0T FSI engine, the 1.9L "pumpe düse" TDI engine and the DSG transmission. For the time, these were all three pretty revolutionary designs.

The only special edition Mk5s are the R32, the Fahrenheit Jetta and GTI and the TDI Cup Edition. Just about all the other Mk5s have a similar station to the Mk3s. They are relatively under-appreciated because of the popularity of the following generation. Many Mk5 Jettas, Rabbits and GTIs can currently be had for a surprisingly low amount of money. For that reason, I would have to say they also make great first cars for a beginner Volkswagen enthusiast. The FSI engine gets kind of a bad rap due to reliability issues with the camshafts and the high-pressure fuel pump. Luckily, this is something that can be pretty quickly inspected before purchase and, unless you are discussing >250 horsepower, these parts last a pretty long time with the proper maintenance. It would be hard for a new VW enthusiast to go wrong with a reasonably low-mileage Mk5 Jetta GLI or GTI with full service history. You simply can't beat the car for the money.

One quick point on these cars is the 2.5L five cylinder engine. It is extraordinarily reliable with the proper maintenance. Although it isn't chosen often by enthusiasts for performance applications or show cars, you won't find a much more reliable daily driver than a 2.5L Rabbit or Jetta. For the most part, you pretty much change oil every 5,000 miles, put gas in them and go. This would be the car of choice for an inexpensive daily driver or the car I'd choose for a problem-free drive across the country. Just like a manual transmission 2.0L Mk3, you simply can't beat a manual transmission 2.5L Mk5 for ultra-reliable transportation.

Ahhhh, the Mk6. The first thing that should be pointed out is the divergence of the German-built Golf based Mk6 and the Mexican-built Jetta based Mk6 in the U.S. This is the first time that the Golf and Jetta have shared very few components and have had different wheelbases. In the U.S. we received the Golf and GTI in late 2009 as a 2010 model, and the Jetta came about a year later as a 2011 model. There are the two and four door Golf and GTI, the Jetta Sportwagon (which is actually based on the Golf), the Tiguan, Eos, and the Golf R. On the Jetta side, there's the Jetta, Jetta GLI and the Jetta Hybrid - all four doors.

Personally, I have had a TDI 2013 Jetta and a 2014 Wolfsburg Edition GTI, and they are both fantastic cars. Each one has its strengths and weaknesses, but I've enjoyed both. The quality, on the whole, for all of the Mk6 vehicles is outstanding. You really can't go wrong using any one of these as a daily driver or show car. 2011 through 2013 non-GLI Jettas have a solid rear axle beam which doesn't particularly lend itself to performance applications; starting in 2014, the Jetta came standard with independent rear suspension.

Beginning with some late Mk5 vehicles and continuing into the Mk7, the TDI engine is the 2.0L common-rail diesel. This has been plagued with controversy, which I won't speak to here. However, if you are into diesel engines, it's worth taking some time just to read up on this engine by itself. It is really quite amazing technology. My Jetta TDI had an incredible amount of torque and incredible fuel mileage. This is a fantastic engine for a daily driver. There is increasing support in the aftermarket for performance modifications, and I feel like it's only a matter of time until people pull off some pretty incredible engine swaps into the earlier chassis (the same goes for the 2.0 TSI gasoline engine).

The main thing with the Mk6, like any generation, is deciding what's important to you upfront. Do I want/ need two or four doors? Do I prefer gas or diesel? What will the car primarily be used for? Do I want/need a manual, automatic or DSG transmission? It'll be a lot easier if you make this decision up front (before car shopping) and then don't compromise.

As of this writing, the Mk7 Golf and GTI were only recently released. They have been designed on Volkswagen's new "MQB" platform that will be the basis for most of its models going forward. I was lucky enough to put the GTI through its paces at the Atlanta Motor Speedway before it was released. Keep in mind I drive a Mk6 GTI every day. This car completely blew me away. The handling is like nothing I've ever experienced in a stock hatchback. The "progressive steering" is incredible. The acceleration and responsiveness are unbelievable. The new 2.0 turbo engine doesn't have an exhaust manifold. (Yes you read that correctly.) Simply put, the Mk7 exceeds the Mk6 in almost every way imaginable (unless you prefer the styling of the Mk6).

Since these vehicles are so new, there are only a handful of modifications available so far, and they've only been represented in small numbers at recent car shows, but this is getting ready to change in a big way I'm sure. If you're the type of person that likes to have cutting edge technology, this is the car for you. If you simply have to have the latest and greatest, this is the car for you. If you want to have a completely custom car no one else has for the time being, this is the car for you. Granted, that is destined to change eventually, but for now, this is the hottest car to have.

That's it for my brief synopsis of the different generations of water-cooled VWs and thanks for sticking with me and not skipping to the next chapter. I'd like to finish with a word to the "I've got to be different" crowd. If you haven't figured it out by now, I'm of the opinion that you should drive whatever the hell you want to drive. There is no wrong answer as far as I'm concerned. Some cars are easier to acquire, cheaper or more popular, and some, well, aren't. For those of you that sincerely want something that virtually nobody has, more power to you. This book is not meant to be an all-inclusive list. If you read this book and go on to build a 914, 924, 928, 964, Mercedes, E30, Thing, Type 34 Ghia, Audi Fox, Corvair, Postal Jeep, put a non-VW engine in a VW, put a VW engine in a non-VW, turn a Beetle into a drift car, slam a Vanagon, ride from the Atlantic to the Pacific on an aircooled VW-powered motorcycle it doesn't matter. Kudos for expressing yourself and not letting anyone tell you what to do. The Volkswagen crowd (for the most part) is very accepting of different tastes. Hopefully you will take something of value away from this book. If you read this book and go on to build an aired-out Routan or common-rail VW-powered Honda CRX and see me at a show, stop me and I'll probably throw you a high-five and buy you a beer.

Acquiring a Car

Now you know who's going to work on your car and you know *where* you're going to work on your own car. You also have a pretty good idea of what kind of car you want to buy. The next step is figuring out the best way to pick one up. This chapter is really all about value. Unless you are independently wealthy, you trade your freedom in one way or another to earn money. This chapter is about getting the best car you can for the least amount of money.

I will begin with cars that are approximately 10 or more model years old. If you're looking to buy a car that's more than about 10 years old, for the most part, you will be buying it from a private party, not a used car lot or dealership.

I have had the best luck over the years buying cars from people I know or "friends of friends". If you have a circle of friends and family who are enthusiasts, I would start by asking around if anyone knows anyone that has the type of car you are looking for. After that, I would extend it out a little bit farther and ask around at a parts store, repair shop or car club. If you don't know anyone selling the type of car you are looking for, the next best place to look is the internet.

If you're looking for something fairly common like a Mk4 Jetta or B5 Passat, I would start on Craigslist. This is the quickest and easiest way to find cars close to you and to start getting an idea of what price people are asking for the car you're looking for. All you have to do is enter the model name and a range of years, for example "Jetta" and "1998-2005". Keep in mind as you start looking that the prices people are asking are the prices people want to get for their car, but in most cases you can usually negotiate the price down once you've looked at the car.

If you're looking for something a little less common - say a Mk3 Jetta TDI or a Mk1 Rabbit GTI - the next best place to look is probably the classified section at the internet forum at vwvortex.com. This is the largest internet forum for water-cooled Volkswagens. I've been using it since the late 90s, and it has been extremely useful for me in many ways over the years. I will come back to VWvortex in more detail later on, but for right now, this is a great resource for finding slightly harder to find cars.

It's not all-inclusive, but a site that I find very useful is searchtempest.com. You have to be kind of broad with your search terms, but it will allow you to search different cities' Craigslist sites and eBay within a radius of a certain zip code.

If you're looking for something very uncommon or specific and you've exhausted Craigslist and VWvortex, another option I've had occasional luck with is www.thesamba.com/vw/. The Samba is primarily an air-cooled internet forum. It's a fantastic resource for air-cooled information, but it does have a water-cooled section in its classifieds and occasionally you'll find some rare cars on there. Another option is eBay. I've bought and sold a handful of cars on eBay and have never had any issues. The rarest of the rare cars usually get sold at auction so that the seller can get the maximum price that the market will allow. If you're in the market for something rare or a car that's 25+ years old with less than 50,000 miles, you will probably have to look to eBay or a similar auction site.

Once you've found a car or cars that you want to go look at, you need to get some kind of idea in your mind about what a fair price is for the car. If you're looking at a more common car, your search will turn up a bunch of similar cars, so you might already have an idea of what a fair market price is for the car. If you're looking for a less common car, it might be hard to figure out the right value for the car. One way to do this is to "watch" several auctions on eBay for similar cars and see what the cars actually sold for. Another way to help figure out car values are online guides or "book values". There are many of these out there, but two of the most popular are NADA and Kelly Blue Book. You input information about the vehicle, and the sites will give you market values for your area based on condition. (NADA even has a classic car section.)

The next step is to contact the person and set up a time to go look at the car. I recommend doing this as quickly as possible. If the car is priced low or it's a particularly nice car, it's not unusual for a car to sell the same day it was posted. This is the point where I would make sure the person has a "clean" title (not reconstructed) in their name. If they do not have this or there is a fishy story about this, walk away. Laws are different in different states, but in most states it will be difficult or impossible for you to get a title at all after purchasing a car if the previous owner didn't have one. Also, if the car has a "reconstructed title", that decimates the value of the car. I would absolutely steer clear of missing or reconstructed titles unless you really know what you are doing. This is different in different parts of the country, so consult your local DMV *before* even considering something like this.

If the ad doesn't mention how the person would like to be paid, this would be a good time to ask. Most private party sellers won't accept personal checks or money orders. The most popular forms of payment are certified bank checks and cash. In some states, you need to meet at a title office or DMV office to transfer titles. In other states, the person can sign over the title and you can take it to the DMV later. Some need to be notarized, some need a bill of sale, etc. Again, I would contact your local DMV and find out the best way to handle this before starting to look at cars.

Before going further in the car-buying discussion, I'd like to pause for a minute and cover a couple brief topics about buying a new car. Buying a new (or recent model year pre-owned) car is pretty straight-forward. I don't plan to take a deep dive into the process of buying a new Volkswagen. There are countless books and internet and magazine articles on this topic. The thing I do want to cover goes back to the part about building a relationship and building trust. One recommendation on buying a new car would be to purchase and service your new Volkswagen at the same dealership. Some people will drive 25 (or 100!) miles away to save $2 per month on their payment and then have the car serviced right up the street from their house. There are several reasons I wouldn't recommend this. One easy example is that some extended warranties have $0 deductible if you take the car back to the selling dealer, but perhaps a $100 deductible at any other dealer. Again, I don't plan to look at every single variable, but from my experience, it's best to purchase and service your car at the same dealership. Maybe the one you like the best is the one 25 miles away, in which case I would consider purchasing and servicing it there.

Another point I'd like to make on purchasing a newer Volkswagen (especially if you plan to modify it) is how friendly the dealership is to modifications. Do they do any in-house modifications or tuning? When you modify your car while it's still under warranty, you invariably void specific components from warranty coverage. If you have a problem while you're under warranty, how likely is it that the dealer will work to determine whether or not the modification caused the issue? I would ask if they've run into these kinds of issues before. At the end of the day, if you modify your car while it's under warranty, sometimes you simply need to "pay to play" when something goes wrong. On the other hand, if a part simply goes bad due to a manufacturer's defect, not because of your engine tune or lowering springs or LED bulbs, etc. it should be covered by your warranty. There are no guarantees here; I would just do your best to find a dealership that will at least work with you if a situation like this comes up. Again, your friends, a car club or VWvortex can go a long way to advise you here.

That's as far as I want to go with new cars. Back to the process of buying an older (10+ model years or so) Volkswagen. You've done some kind of a search and have found one or more cars that you'd like to go look at. Don't overthink this part. Unless you have very high standards, you will probably only need to go look at two or three cars, tops, before working out a deal. All your research should have been done *before* the point when you're ready to go look at cars. Also, as a lifelong enthusiast, I'd also politely request that you be respectful of other people and their time. Please don't waste an hour or two of someone's time just to kick the tires, have a conversation and go for a quick drive. Unless something surprising turns up while you are looking the car over, you should know pretty quickly if it's the right car for you and what you're willing to pay. Please have some empathy for the other person.

If you or a friend or family member have enough mechanical expertise, you can go look at the car yourself and determine if it's the right car for you and approximately the right price to pay. If you don't have this knowledge or aren't as confident, another great option is to ask the seller if it would be OK to take the car to a dealership or repair shop to have it inspected before you purchase it. I would call your dealership or repair shop and ask them ahead of time if they can do this, whether you need an appointment and how much they charge (usually about $75-$125 dollars). Have this information ready before you reach out to a seller, and let them know early on in the conversation that you would like to have the car inspected before buying it. You, as the buyer, will likely be responsible for the cost of the inspection, but I would say that it is *money well spent*. A professional technician who works on cars like yours every day will be able to let you know about most potential issues *before* you purchase the car instead of finding out the hard way *after*. If this type of inspection is important to you and the seller won't accommodate it, it's probably a good sign that you should find a different car.

If you or someone you know is confident enough to inspect the car yourself, this next bit is for you. When you're going to look at a car, you are trying to assess what condition it's in versus other cars for sale in the market. What you are looking for are any value-added things (complete maintenance history, "one owner" cars, desirable accessories and modifications, etc.) but also things about the car that detract from the value (rust, worn out tires, a fishy or missing title, etc.) My first piece of advice would be to only look at a car during the daytime on a sunny day. Looking at a car in the dark or while it is wet or snowy outside will hide a lot of flaws.

The first step when looking at a car is to visually inspect the car. This will weed out some cars quickly so you aren't wasting your or the other person's time. Does the paint look like the original paint? If it's been repainted, how good of a job does it appear to be? If you know ahead of time that rust is a non-starter for you (which it is for a lot of people), lie down on the ground and look at the underside of the car and inside the fender wells before you do much of anything else. On the earlier cars, pay close attention to the strut towers under the hood and the part of the body where the rear suspension mounts. Another revealing place to look is under the carpet in the trunk. Any signs of major impact or rust back here are a bad sign. Rust, bad bodywork and structural damage are some of the worst things to combat for an enthusiast. Some minor rust, dings or dents are going to be unavoidable, particularly the older the car is. That said, I don't care how "rare" a car is. If you aren't equipped with the skills to cut out major rust and weld in new panels or fix someone else's shoddy bodywork, move on to a different car. There are so many "builds" and "projects" that eventually get sold or scrapped because the owner doesn't realize that they're in way over their head until it's too late.

I've never seen someone do it, but I've always thought it would be a good idea to bring your own checklist of things to inspect on the car. Experienced enthusiasts can take a pretty quick look at a car, make some mental notes and know what they should pay for the car. If you're less experienced, it can be really hard to process all that information at one time. It might help to write it down as you go. For example, "Needs tires - $400" or "Has cat-back exhaust + $200". This will help you tally the pros and cons and help you figure out a fair price to pay for the car.

Next, I would look at the wheels and tires. Inspect for any damage, the amount of tread left and any signs of obvious uneven treadwear (which might point to bigger issues in the steering or suspension). Are they the correct original wheels for the car, have they been replaced or are they aftermarket? After that, I would look under the hood. Does the car appear to have the original engine or has it been replaced? Do you see major fluid leaks or evidence of fishy wiring? Fire it up and listen to it. Does it start quickly without a struggle? Is it smooth at idle and responsive when you press on the gas? The best case scenario is to start the engine after it has been sitting for a while (preferably overnight) and let it get warmed up all the way. This is an easy thing to breeze over without thinking, but you would hate to part with your hard-earned cash only to find out that your new baby is hard to start when it's cold or has an overheating problem when all the way warmed up.

Try *everything* inside the car. Does the heat work? What about the air conditioning? The radio? All the seatbelts, all the windows, all the door locks, the glovebox - you get the idea. Some issues here might not be a big deal to you (perhaps the power door locks don't work or the radio doesn't work), but other things could be a big deal (no air conditioning in the South or heat/ defrost in the North). If the seller says something like, "The odometer stopped at 90,000 miles, but I would guess it's got about 105,000 miles," look at the seats and carpet. Do they look like they've got 105,000 miles worth of wear or 250,000 miles?

At this point the seller has probably figured out that you are more knowledgeable and/or thorough than the average car buyer. Just the act of being this thorough will probably nudge him or her to offer up problems with the car that they might not have brought up otherwise. Make mental notes or write down any issues you find. This will come back into play when deciding whether or not to buy the car and negotiating the price.

The next and most important step is to *test drive the car*. If you are buying a project car that doesn't run, then this obviously doesn't apply. For *everything* else, *test drive the car*. I am not a legal expert or insurance expert and I know different laws and rules apply in different places, so you will need to research this part separately before you go to look at a car. Ideally, it should be you driving, not the owner. Whose insurance is primary if you get in a wreck? Who's allowed to drive? Call your insurance company and local DMV and let them know what your plans are and ask what you should do in advance. That said, there are so many things that you can notice driving the car that you simply can't without.

Does the transmission shift smoothly? Does the suspension feel firm and free of noises? Does the steering feel firm and free of noises? etc. If you or someone you know isn't qualified to determine this, go back to the step where you should have a dealership or repair shop inspect the car for you. Do the turn signals work? Do the brakes feel firm and responsive? Does the transmission grind into any gears? Does the clutch slip? etc.

By this time you should have a pretty clear picture in your head of the history of the car, any issues it has, whether or not you want to buy it and, if so, what an appropriate price to pay would be (adding or deducting for anything you've just found). This book isn't about negotiating skills or how to flip cars. There are countless other resources on those topics. What I will tell you is that you never want to pay over fair market value for a car unless it is ultra-rare or truly one-of-a-kind. That said, you will rarely be able to pay significantly less than fair market value for a running-driving car, so going to look at a bunch of cars in hopes of low-balling everyone will probably end up being a waste of yours and several other people's time. If you've done your due diligence, then make an offer a little lower than what you think is fair and take it from there. Any price at or below the market value is a good deal, so don't stress out about this. The more important thing is that you are getting the right car in the right condition at a fair price. I would rather have the car I always wanted at a fair price than compromise on the car because it's a "great deal".

After you've agreed to buy the car, don't get too excited just yet and miss out on a few important details. Make sure you exchange the title (in whatever way is required in your state) for payment at the same time. Ask if the car has any other keys, paperwork, window sticker, maintenance records, repair manuals, floor mats, spare parts, etc. that come with it before finalizing the deal. Once the title is transferred, it is your car and the seller doesn't owe you anything, so make sure you ask any questions you might have beforehand.

Unless you plan to park the car and turn it into a full-on project, the next step will be to register and insure the car. It's a good idea to do this immediately before even driving the car. In many states, you will probably need to have the car inspected before you can register it, so you may want to find out what you need to do beforehand. Keep in mind all the title transfer, registration, insurance, inspection, property tax costs when budgeting also. Some states will issue some kind of a temporary transport tag to allow you to transport the car home or to an inspection station. This would be a good choice for a lot of people, but you will need to get one before trying to drive the car.

After purchasing a car, most people's first instinct is to run right out and purchase a bunch of accessories or do a bunch of repairs right away. I would advise against this. By all means, take care of any safety-related repairs. Give the car a good cleaning. Change the oil and filter. Replace the tires or brakes if they're unsafe. Replace the wiper blades if they're not working correctly. Do anything required to pass a state inspection, but I would temporarily stop there. Drive the car. Put some miles on it over the course of a few days or weeks and make sure there aren't any unforeseen issues or things you maybe didn't notice when buying the car. I like to make a list of all the issues I find on my cars as well as a list of potential modifications I might want to do. The only way you can make a comprehensive and accurate list is by driving the car several times and getting a feel for it. This advice applies even to the most experienced enthusiasts who might be quick to skip it.

A lot of people run into a bad situation by buying an older car and immediately repainting it or adding expensive wheels or expensive engine modifications, only to find out the underlying mechanics of the car need attention. You might run into a situation where you had a short-term budget of, say, $1500 to spend on the car and you run right out and buy lowering springs and a set of wheels only to find out a few weeks later you need to have the alternator replaced. This is a very important takeaway. Give yourself a little bit of time to get used to the car and make a list of anything that you might want to address or modify. Only then can you make a level-headed game-plan for the order in which you want to tackle everything and approximately how much it's going to cost. To really drive this point home...as soon as buy the car, you will be tempted to buy new floor-mats or replace the timing belt or the whole ignition system or buy air-ride or new wheels or a new stereo. Don't do it. Wait a little bit. It's called delayed gratification and, in this case, *it almost always pays off.*

This short cooling-off period would be a good time to start learning as much as you can about your car. If it didn't come with an owner's manual, this would be a good time to pick one up (this sounds boring or pedestrian, but you might be surprised). On newer models, you can still pick one up from the dealership, or for all models try eBay, Amazon or the classified section at VWvortex. Unless you plan to have someone else do every bit of work to your car, you will need a repair manual. Bentley manuals are generally considered to be the gold standard for repair manuals, at least for the older cars. They are the most accurate and comprehensive. If one is available for your car, it will be a completely invaluable asset. You don't need to sit down and read it cover to cover, but I would take this time to at least familiarize yourself with it so you know right where to go when you do need it. A lot of technical questions by new VW owners will quickly be met with, "Check the Bentley manual and come back if you still have any questions." I wouldn't say I hoard them, but I personally wouldn't own an older water-cooled VW without having a matching Bentley manual. Don't think you're saving a few bucks by picking up another brand of manual. You will most likely run into something that isn't covered in your manual that is in a Bentley manual. If you do need to feed that consumer fix of buying something for your car right away, this would be at the top of my list.

One more point I'd like to make about finding a car is that you may not always be able to work out a deal and take a car home on the first visit. Sometimes it takes time and persistence. Sometimes, it might take months or years of persistence. If you really want the car but just can't make a deal, find a way to keep in touch with the person. Some of the best deals I've gotten have come after I've kept up with someone for a while only for them to have a change of heart and sell me the car in the end.

There are three main reasons someone might change their mind. The first is that the person simply wanted too much money for the car initially. After a while of not selling the car at the desired price, they might be willing to entertain a lower offer, or they might simply have to sell and accept a lower price. The second reason is that they might have plans to do some major mechanical or body work to the car first before selling the car to command full price. Sometimes, people simply don't get this done whether they're in over their head or just lose interest. The third main reason is that someone might be too attached to the car and when they're actually faced with someone trying to buy it they just can't let their car go. Maybe they've owned it for a very long time or it's been in the family for a long time or has other sentimental value. A top tip would be to periodically keep in touch with these people. Many times, nothing more will come from it. Sometimes, you'll make a friend out of the situation. Sometimes, though, the person will change their mind and you could end up with a really great car at a great price and maybe even a new friend on top of all of that. (I've had this happen myself - it can be a win-win-win.)

If you're interested in racing, I'm sorry but I won't be including much information on purpose-built race cars because I don't have much personal experience with the topic. There are books on this topic and if this is your primary interest, these people are pretty welcoming to newcomers. I would start by going to your next area autocross, drag race or local VW speed shop. There are a lot of people that can help point you in the right direction. The next two chapters are about the "scene" and the spectrum from daily driver to show cars. The next two chapters will be my attempt to roughly split enthusiast's cars into two sections. Chapter Six will be about cars intended for daily-driver use. Chapter Seven will be about non-daily-driven cars used as a second, weekend, or occasional show car. Feel free to skip a chapter that you feel doesn't apply to you, but I think most people would get a lot of value from reading right through the whole thing. I hope some part of the next two chapters speaks directly to you, personally.

The Daily Driver

Most of the Volkswagens I have owned were in this category. Some were completely stock and some were pretty heavily modified, but I've driven most of my cars every day. It sounds obvious, but it may not be; most VW enthusiasts I know drive a Volkswagen every day. For newer cars, it's not so hard to make that happen. You fill it with gas, perform maintenance every so often and it keeps reliably going every time you need it. However, driving an older Volkswagen to school or work every day is a commitment. You will figure out that older Volkswagens (older cars in general) are more obviously machines. They can and at times will be temperamental or simply will not work. Driving an older Volkswagen every day isn't basic transportation; it is unquestionably a lifestyle. This is why I have to say I am more impressed by the person fighting the constant battle every day against entropy with their 1979 Rabbit than the Mk6 with air-ride and expensive three-piece wheels.

I am not knocking the choice to daily drive a modern car with modern reliability and creature comforts. This is actually what I have been doing for the last four years or so. It's just that driving an old Volkswagen every day isn't a rational decision. It's a visceral statement that your car is an expression of who you are or what you think you're about. The key here though is reliability. It's fun cruising to work in your Mk2, but it's something else when you find yourself late to work because your car won't start. All decisions made about your daily driver should start with the question, "How will this affect my car's reliability?"

Should you install coil-overs and adjust them almost all the way down without helper springs on your daily-driven Mk4? Only if you don't mind not being able to drive down some roads, breaking your oil pan (probably more than once and risking damaging your engine), wearing out your tires in a quarter of their normal life and repeatedly replacing broken axles. This is just one hyper-specific example, but there are a handful of people out there that live this lifestyle every day. Again, your car may look super cool rolling down the road, but this is not at all what I would recommend for a daily driver.

There are a lot of modifications that can be done to a Volkswagen that don't compromise (and sometimes even enhance) its reliability. It's not hard to accessorize or mildly modify your car to express your personality without having to worry much about getting where you're going. Before we even get into common modifications/accessories though, you need to make sure you're starting with a solid enough foundation. The key here is making sure your car is running optimally and safely. If you run right out and start modifying a car that has underlying issues, you won't know if, for example, your engine tune is causing a misfire or if it's your worn out spark plugs that you never inspected. You won't know if your lowering springs are causing a noise or if it's a bad strut or bushing that you never inspected. In the name of safety, reliability and saving you or your mechanic a ton of headaches, *make sure your car is running properly, caught up on recommended maintenance and that all potential safety issues are addressed first*. I know, there's that delayed gratification again, but your wallet, your safety and your (or your mechanic's) sanity will thank me later.

Start with the basics. Change the oil and filter. Make sure your car passes your state's safety inspection. Make sure your tires have enough tread to be safe. If it's due and you have no history of it being done, replace your timing belt and water pump. This is where I start when I purchase an older car I plan to daily. (Car people use daily as a verb if you haven't heard it before.) I change the oil and filter, do whatever is needed to pass state inspection, replace the timing belt if there's no history and if it's a higher mileage car, make sure the heat and air conditioning work and there are no scary noises. Next, I start driving the car every day for a few days or weeks to get familiar with it and find any other potential issues I might have overlooked. My goal is to have a car that will start every single time I try to start it without issue, run reliably without risk of stalling or overheating and get the fuel mileage and performance it is supposed to be getting.

While this is going on, I'm starting to paint a picture in my head of what I want the car to look like. This is unique to every driver. For me, the first things I usually want to do are lower the car, install bigger/wider wheels, window tint and a good radio if the car doesn't have one. For someone else, it might be a cold-air intake, cat-back exhaust, engine tune and performance tires. Another person might want to install speakers and a subwoofer and vinyl wrap the car.

In the words of author and speaker Stephen Covey, you need to "begin with the end in mind." This is true in many parts of life, but I find it to be particularly helpful with car projects. Before you even begin to modify your car, you should be able to roughly visualize what it will look like when it is finished. Then you can start taking concrete steps toward that visualized goal. Some people with artistic skills can sit down and simply draw what their car will look like when finished. I don't have those skills. I usually do this by working with one of the various apps that will allow you to see what different modifications look like on your car (Mk1 Modifier, Dubmodder, etc.) Also, I'll search the internet for cars that are similar to what I want mine to look like and bookmark them. This is especially helpful because in the process of looking for cars that you like, you will find interesting threads about what people did to their car and maybe some pitfalls to avoid. You might also meet some like-minded people and make friends along the way.

OK, so you have a visual idea of what you want your car to look like when done. The next step is figuring out what concrete steps you need to take to get there. This is where I make a list. I list the things I want to do to the car in order of descending importance, and then I list the approximate cost for each item next to it. I do this on a Google Doc so I can update it whenever/wherever I want to. This is especially helpful if I'm actually driving the car and I realize I need some random small part for the car and I want to write it down before I forget it. Pencil and paper is fine too, but I find it easier to maintain on my cell phone. The important thing is actually making the list and realizing that it's a working document that you'll be removing items from once they're finished and adding items that you might not have thought about.

The next step is making a budget and a timeline goal. I'm going to make up some numbers. For a daily driver, say all the things on your list total up to $1500 - $3000. Is that money that you already have available to spend, or will you have to save and gradually tick things off your list over time? What timeline do you have in mind? Can you set aside $300 per month and be finished in 5-10 months? This is completely up to you, but it's important to have a budget and a timeline. Whatever your budget and timeline are, you should add 50%. I have no specific data to support that number, but you will *always* have unforeseen expenses in a project car. Also, you probably lead a pretty busy life, and a lot of people tend to be overconfident when predicting how much time they can dedicate to their car. It's important to be honest with yourself up front so you don't end up disappointed later.

Another thing to consider when budgeting time and money is an old hot-rod phrase I love. I don't know where it came from or who to give credit to, but it's, "Money, time and speed. You can pick two." I think it could also be phrased, "Money, time and quality. You can pick two." This is true if you're working on your own car, but even more so if someone else is doing the work. Quality work takes lots of time and money. If you want something done quickly and with high quality, it's going to cost a lot of money. If you want something high quality and cheap, it's going to take a long time. If you want something cheap and quick, it's going to be low quality. I've found this to be almost universally true. Please keep it in mind when you're making plans and especially when dealing with shops or dealerships.

The slippery slope a lot of people find themselves on is a result of not having a goal in mind when they start. Sometimes, this is not so bad, but other times it can be really painful. I will give you a couple of examples:

Joe buys a four door Mk3 Golf to daily. He's a single guy, lives with some friends who are also car guys and earns enough money to be able to spend money on his car regularly. He spends most of his free time either driving or working on the car. He starts out lowering it, then puts some wheels on it. He finds some Euro bumpers for it, and then puts rear disc brakes on it. Joe's starting to have a pretty fun, reliable little car. Then, a roommate comes across a wrecked Mk1 Audi TT. Joe decides to buy the TT and park the Golf and swap the engine, transmission, dash, seats, etc. to the Golf. This turns into a longer-term project and Joe needs to find a new daily while he works on the Golf.

Chris buys a Mk2 16v GTI. Chris just moved in with his girlfriend and got married. They both work and earn a decent living. He has a basic level of mechanical experience and does a lot of research online. He starts out installing a cup kit suspension, wheels and tires, and a full length exhaust system. Then he decides to put high performance cams in one long weekend. He quickly realizes he doesn't have all the tools he needs and is having trouble timing the cams. Sunday turns into Monday and he and his wife decide to carpool for a week until he can finish installing the cams. Another weekend goes by and he still can't get the job finished. Now things are starting to get tense and he's considering towing the car to a shop to have the job finished, but that will be pretty expensive. The following Tuesday, Chris finds out they're going to have a baby. What should be joyful, happy news turns into stressful news because now Chris can't afford to pay a shop to put his GTI back together. He's left with having to buy another car or unload the GTI for less than it's worth because it's not running.

Sometimes, like in the first example, not having a plan can work out fine because you may have a lot of time, help or resources. More often, I feel, not having a plan can leave you in a bad spot or even disaster. This part isn't meant to scare you; it's meant to remind you that life is inherently unpredictable and at the end of the day, when we're talking about a daily driver, it needs to be *reliable*.

Some of the most popular accessories and modifications that don't have a big effect on reliability are wheels and tires, mild lowering springs, mild engine tunes, intake systems, mild exhaust systems, European lighting, European or aftermarket bumpers or fender flares, upgraded or aftermarket radio. You get the idea. The bottom line is that they are all intended to personalize or enhance the car without diminishing *reliability* in any major way. Any project you plan to tackle should ideally be able to be completed by yourself or a shop in a day or two and have you right back on the road. There are still ways to be creative with your car without affecting reliability. I've seen impressive paint jobs, bigger brakes, different front ends, different seats, different steering wheels - you name it - but they all don't have a big impact on *reliability*.

A daily driver also has to fit your needs. When I was younger, before I had kids, I was living in an apartment complex and had about a 12-mile commute to work at a VW dealership. I traded for a Mk1 Cabriolet with a 2.0 16v with side-draft carbs, a header and an almost straight-pipe exhaust. To this day, it was probably the quickest and most exhilarating VW I've ever owned. It had a racing seat with a five-point harness and no passenger seat. Imagine, for a second, how my neighbors must have felt when I fired up that fire-breathing monster every morning at about 6:45 a.m. Even just trying to idle it out of the apartment complex was completely obnoxious.

Imagine the 12-mile commute with no heat and an unsprung clutch in stop-and-go traffic. Imagine how pissed off my ex-wife was the handful of times she had to ride in the back seat as I drove like a maniac with her fingers pressed in her ears. Imagine the handful of times it started to misfire on the way to work and I had to diagnose whether it was the carbs or an ignition problem in a small parking lot with limited tools. Imagine how scared I was the time one of the fuel lines split and started spraying fuel all over the hot exhaust. Luckily, I never got myself in any real trouble, but I just as easily could have lost my job, burned my car to the ground, been kicked out of my apartment or killed. It would have been the ultimate second car, and I wish I'd realized that at the time, but it made for a horribly unreliable daily driver. Daily drivers need to be at least somewhat practical, and they absolutely must be reliable. If you compromise on this point, it will be to your peril. Practicality and reliability.

Project & Show Cars

For almost my entire adult life I've had a second car to tinker with. Often, they've not been very expensive, but they've allowed me to get the tinkering out of my system without affecting the reliability of my daily driver. This is the sweet spot in my opinion. A reliable, modern daily driver and an older project car. Not everyone has the means to make this happen. I know a lot of young people who simply can't afford it and after the recession a lot of older people had to give up this lifestyle. If you can manage it, though, I think this is the way to go for most people. Some people do the opposite and drive an older, cheaper but reliable car every day and buy a modern car to modify or show. The age of the car doesn't matter. The important thing is having a reliable car to get you where you need to go and a second car to do whatever you want without the stress of worrying about getting to school or work.

For the second car, the opportunities are endless, but a new set of questions arise. Do you have a place to store it, preferably out of the elements? If you plan to drive it to shows or events, what needs to be done for it to be inspected and registered and insured? If you have the means to trailer it to shows, will you skip the registration? If it's a dedicated show car or classic car that you won't drive much, does it qualify for classic car insurance?

If you don't plan to drive a car much, I would recommend you look into specialized insurance for your second (or third, etc.) car. I had classic car insurance on my '77 Rabbit and now on my '61 Beetle. Since I park them in the garage all the time and only drive them a small handful of times a year to local shows, I save hundreds (will be thousands over the years) of dollars on insurance premiums. Also a lot of these policies have "agreed value". In the event of a total loss, you would receive the agreed value, not market value, and no depreciation. Also, some of these companies will work with you if your car is a project and periodically raise the value of your car if you can demonstrate that you've improved the value. I am by no means an expert, but I think a lot of people might pay way too much for insurance premiums on classic cars, coupled with the potential double whammy if there's a total loss and they're stuck arguing with their insurance company about the value of their car. There are some basics, like it needs to be parked in a garage or covered space, there is a maximum amount of miles you can drive per year, they will require photos of the car at a minimum and they may want to come physically look at the car. All that said, if classic cars are your lifestyle, this is probably the way to go. Personally, I have one policy for my classic car and a separate policy for my other cars.

Drivability. If you won't be able to trailer your car to shows and events and plan to drive it more than a handful of miles, it still needs to be reliably drivable. I've known a handful of people whose modus operandi is repairing their car on the side of the road almost every time they drive to a show. Although this probably isn't the end of the world if you have the skills and tools but not a lot of money, for most people this can be a disaster. Sure, you might end up with some fun stories about the time you had to change a timing belt in a rainstorm on the interstate or had a flat tire but no spare so you had to use someone else's spare, until you had another flat tire then had to try to find a low-profile tire in a town with a population of 1,500. Cars are machines, and they're bound to have problems eventually. Everyone that's been around this lifestyle any length of time has war stories about their car breaking down in some far-away place and having to do something like MacGyver a shifter linkage out of paperclips and nylons. These types of stories will provide laughs and conversation for years, but please, make sure your car is reliable, make sure you have a spare tire, and make sure you have jumper cables and a jack. There are some basics without which you are just setting yourself up for problems.

I'm not as brazen on this topic as I was when I was younger. Nowadays if we're going to an out-of-town show, I will drive the car I'm planning to show and my wife will follow in the Mk6. That way we can bring some basic tools, a good jack, some basic parts like fuses, a cooler, any luggage, etc. One time, my brother and I were driving to SoWo and he had a passenger and I was in my Mk2 GTI with my wife riding passenger. We were each loaded down with all of the above-mentioned stuff. Everything was going fine until a pickup truck ran off the road and totaled my brother's car with his friend in it (luckily he was OK). After we got through dealing with the frustration, the police, towing his car and everything else, we had to cram four people and four people's worth of luggage, tools, coolers and folding chairs into my slammed Mk2 and drive 15 miles to the nearest rental car company and pray they'd rent us a car late on a Friday afternoon. Having a chase car would make this kind of situation so much easier. Sure, you have to use double the gas per show, but unless you're trailering your car, I think it's worth it.

I can tell you that air-cooled, hot-rod and muscle car guys have this figured out. When you go to one of their larger shows, the parking lot looks like an RV convention. The water-cooled scene is not there at all yet, but perhaps one day it will be. If you think about all the money spent on hotels, drives on the highway in 95 degree weather with no AC, constant nagging possibility that your car might have an issue, this would definitely be the way to go. The problem is the barrier of entry is so high. They're very expensive and take up a ton of space. I won't spend a lot of time on this particular item other than to say for the lifers, this might definitely be the direction the water-cooled community should move in. My aunt and uncle had an RV with an enclosed trailer, and figuring out where to book a hotel at a show, whether or not they were going to make it, where to put parts bought at a swap meet, etc. were never an issue.

Another piece of advice on project cars that I think is universal is that for most people, you can only really enjoy them when you're driving them. This may sound obvious, but it gets overlooked all the time. People get hung up on their car needing to be "finished", or they are embarrassed about what it looks like at the moment, or they bite off way more than they can chew and park their car for months or years trying to do too much at once. Most of the fun in having a project car is driving it. Period. As long as it's safe to drive, get it out there and drive it. I bet you'll have a lot more fun and create a lot more really great memories driving your car that is lowered on stock wheels, has the wrong color hood, plasti-dipped or primered, has no interior or whatever, than leaving it at home in the garage waiting for it to be finished. Parking it for the winter and knocking off bite-sized chunks of work is fine, but I've known too many people who go to show after show after show without a car because they're waiting for their car to be finished. *If it's safe to drive, get it out there and drive it.* You won't regret it. If it sits in your garage for two or three or ten years and you never end up finishing it, you will regret it. I promise.

I'd like to make a few quick comments about spouses or significant others and project cars. Number one, how supportive is your significant other of your hobby? I am lucky to be married to a woman who is very supportive, loves going to shows, loves looking at the cars and is respectful of the time it requires for me to be in the garage, working on cars. If your significant other isn't that supportive, I would recommend sitting down immediately and having a discussion. Why aren't they supportive? Is it that you guys simply can't afford to have that kind of hobby right now? Is it that they feel like you don't spend enough time with them? Whatever the reason is, you need to come to some kind of resolution or you are walking on shaky ground and headed for bigger problems.

Another pitfall is the significant other that impulsively purchases something every time you buy something for your car (assuming you are not also being impulsive). This is dangerous because it's not a good investment in your financial health. If you buy yourself a set of three-piece wheels or they come home with, "Surprise!" or "I wanted to treat myself" or "I deserved this", you guys are not communicating properly and are heading down an unwise financial path together. I've heard of this going the other way too where people never "add up the receipts of their build", so when their significant other asks them how much they've spent, they answer with, "I don't know, I haven't added up my receipts." Any type of behavior in this category by either person is headed for disaster. Big financial decisions should be made together with the knowledge and approval of both parties.

Any friction in most relationships begins with lack of honesty or lack of communication. Make sure your significant other is supportive. If not, sit down and talk about why not and try to come to some kind of solution. Don't be selfish or try to keep financial information from them. Be respectful. You don't want to hear criticism about the time you spend on your hobby. Don't be critical of how they spend time on their hobby. Be open and honest and make all big financial decisions together. This is not an all-inclusive list, but I think I covered the primary pitfalls for most car people. Like everything in life, honesty, respect and open communication prevent all types of problems.

Scarcity & Respecting Rare Cars

Many collectors or hobbyists of all types like to use the word "rare". You'll hear it frequently if you start spending time around car people. As of this writing, there isn't much in the water-cooled VW scene that is truly rare (Harlequin Golfs being an exception). Whenever someone calls something rare, it may in fact be be quite common (Mk1 Rabbits), but have become *scarce* because there is a *much greater demand* than *supply*. I'm not trying to correct people's grammar. I am trying to help you understand what people mean, though, for two reasons. The first reason is that if you buy a rare or scarce car, you need to absolutely keep in mind that unless you destroy it, you are its *temporary* caretaker. The second is that all types of people will demand sky-high values when selling all kinds of cars and parts by calling them *rare*.

Let's start with the first point. For one reason or another, there are some types of cars where very few are left or very few are left in excellent condition. I'm mostly talking about cars, but this also applies to specific parts as well. These can sometimes be jokingly called "unobtanium". This could be because very few were made originally (Swallowtail Rabbits), or the specific type of car typically had multiple owners and was used hard its whole life (eg. clean Mk1 GTIs) or because they didn't hold up to the elements (Type 2 Buses).

So you bought a truly rare or scarce car. I get it, it's your car and you're going to do whatever you want. That's fair. If the car is completely rotted out or destroyed by a previous owner, don't let me hold you back. That's not what I'm talking about. I'm talking about anything that could remotely be deemed restorable or roadworthy. To make my point, I'm going to use an example of a 1980 Rabbit Pickup. There were only about 25,000 of these made for the U.S. market. This was also the only year they made the "early Westy" front end. These didn't stand up well to the snow/ice/salt. I'm not sure how many are left nationwide, but I'd guess it's a pretty low number. You've managed somehow to get your hands on a relatively straight, un-molested 1980 "Caddy". I won't criticize anything you want to do to it as long as it can be reversed later on by a future owner. This little truck has managed to survive for 35+ years against the odds. Please don't take the early Westy front end off and install a single-round front end. Please don't turn it into an extended-cab project. Please don't cut the rain tray out. Please don't give up on the project, cut it in half and turn it into a trailer. If it has decent strut towers and the tailgate is there, *someone will put it back on the road.* No criticism of you, personally - don't feel bad - but if you are tempted to modify something like this, please sell it to someone else who will preserve it and find something less scarce to heavily modify.

Hopefully, if you take care of it, you'll eventually be able to sell or pass your car on to someone else who will get to enjoy it for many years after you. Remember, every time one of these vehicles bites the dust, the rest become more and more scarce. It becomes harder and harder for everyone else to get their hands on one. Eventually, the market for scarce water-cooled VWs is probably going to take off similar to the way it has for air-cooled VWs. At that point, you will need to be pretty wealthy to even think about finding a clean, original car. If you need any proof of this, go online and look at what people are willing to pay for rotten early '60s buses. Then go and look at the lengths (amount of metal replacement!) they're willing to go to restore them.

As for "rare" parts, there really aren't that many that are truly rare. Take BBS RS wheels for example - you see them all over the place at car shows and they seem to be everywhere, but they constantly command a high price because there isn't a big enough supply for all the people that want them. The same goes for parts that were fairly abundant in Europe but not sold in America (I'm thinking Euro bumpers, ABF engines, etc.) They aren't rare; there just aren't that many of them in the U.S. to keep up with demand. One of the main types of "rare" water-cooled parts nowadays in the real sense of the word are new/never installed/NOS parts. NOS Mk2 Rallye front end parts and pop-out window kits have gone through the roof in value. The same goes for NOS Mk1 floor mats and accessories. Also, if you ever even come across them, new Oettinger or Drake parts are rare in the true sense of the word.

Don't believe that a certain under-dash knee bar, a specific instrument cluster, a mono-wiper or whatever is rare unless you've been around the hobby for a little while or have a knowledgeable friend to consult first. If you're newer to the scene, I would chalk this up as a trap to avoid. At risk of sounding like a cynic, once in a while I meet someone who wants to show me every little nuanced rare part on their car and I just don't get it. Real gray Mk1 Euro-bumpers will stop me in my tracks whenever I come across them. So will all the parts on a real unmolested Mk2 Rallye Golf, but your one-year-only, uncommon color, non-AC center console might look very nice, but it's not rare in the true sense of the word.

There are people who look for scarce parts in junkyards. I used to do this in high school. You're putting useable parts that were destined for the crusher back in circulation. A person who does this on a regular basis will become one of your best friends. Unless you have a nearly perfect all-original or show-stopping car, what I don't advocate, however, is going online and paying through the nose for that extra-special one-year-only grab handle. There are much better things you could be doing with your money.

Probably the most frustrating thing for me nowadays is the scarce cars that get parted out or cut up to harvest their parts. Cars get parted out and crushed all the time. That's a normal part of the car world. If a car has been in a bad wreck or a fire or is rotted out beyond repair, there's no problem whatsoever. If it's a common car (many Mk4s for example), it's not a problem parting it out even if it could still be put back on the road. The frustrating thing for me is when I see a former show car that stopped running or an early Rabbit that doesn't start getting parted out and crushed. I was guilty of this when I was a teenager. I helped part out a Mk1 GTI and a 16v Scirocco. They were in below-average condition, but could have been put back on the road. Back then, I didn't really understand what this hobby was all about, and I just saw some parts I could sell and make a little money from. Please don't do this. Make your best effort to sell the whole car or at least the shell to someone that will put it back on the road.

I continuously see people claiming that cars are "too far gone". I'm not there in person to look at the car, so I don't know for sure, but I look at the pictures and I'm blown away at the cars people are parting out because they're "too far gone". I can't tell if these people haven't been around the scene that long or if they're using it as an easy excuse to turn a big profit parting out cars. I think, as a group, we need to work together to slow this down. Obviously anyone saying a car is "too far gone" has no plans to put it back on the road. The first thing we can try to do, collectively, is point out that it's not that bad and they should really try to attempt to sell the whole car or at least the shell to someone who could put it back on the road.

The second thing we can do is boycott anyone who repeatedly junks useable, reasonably rare cars to turn a profit. If you see someone (they're not hard to spot) repeatedly cutting up Mk1s so they can have a huge inventory of hard-to-find parts to profit from, you need to stop buying those parts. I know it's hard because the parts are so hard to find in the first place, but we're allowing someone to permanently decrease the supply of our favorite cars and drive up the prices for parts in the meantime. This does *not* include people cutting up abundant cars or cars that truly are too far gone. I'm talking about the person who is cutting up a Rabbit pickup because it doesn't run and "no one will give them enough for it" or a VR6 Mk3 GTI because of a bad transmission. If the body is scrap, fine. But if the body is in fair condition, the car should be put back on the road, period. Any effort to cut these types of cars up hurts the community as a whole.

The Internet

Like everything else, the car enthusiast community has been changed forever with the rise of the internet. Parts availability used to be limited to dealerships, local shops and mail-order catalogs. Now you can check availability and order parts from all over the globe without even having to make a phone call. In the past, the most advice you could get was that of friends, local car clubs and shops. Now you can literally get advice from people all over the globe, instantaneously. Shopping for a classic car used to be limited to the local newspaper, automotive classified magazines (I used to love poring over these magazines until my fingers were covered in newsprint ink). Now you can search online for a car on your phone without even having to get out of bed in the morning. Every kind of change has its benefits and drawbacks. I think most people would agree that the internet has mostly been beneficial to the car community, but it also has some specifically annoying drawbacks.

I remember when I was a teenager having to wait all month until the next issue of *Performance VW* or *Hot VWs* came out so I could see the latest builds and how-to articles. Now people get Instafamous all the time, and you can see about as much (or as little) as you want of what's going on in the car community instantly. Not only can I see the wheels you just ordered for your build, but I also get to see the burrito you ate for lunch after you got done installing them.

What I'm getting at is that there is an absolutely endless amount of information online and a new level of interconnectedness that never used to be possible. I will try to detail some of what I think are the most beneficial internet tools and some sage advice about who (and who not) to listen to. Keep in mind this section by definition won't be timeless. New internet companies, blogs, apps and online communities sprout up all the time.

What I'm going for is to draw a rough sketch of what the internet means to the VW community as of this writing so you can become familiar if you aren't already.

Internet forums have become one of the most valuable parts of the online VW community. There are a bunch out there but overwhelmingly, the most popular water-cooled forum is vwvortex.com. There are also some really great, although more specific, forums, like TDI Club and Stanceworks, for example. If you're looking for a place to start learning about VWs and networking online, though, VWvortex is a great all-purpose place to start. It's organized into loads of sub-categories so you can get as specific as you like.

My top advice for participating in online VW forums is to keep in mind that they are typically double-edged swords. There is a lot of information, but not all (and sometimes very little) of it is accurate or helpful. Imagine that a VW forum is a forum for people who have or are interested in learning about a specific medical condition. The discussion would mostly be people's subjective experiences and opinions.

Sure, there'd be some science, but a lot of the discussion might not be accurate, scientific, actionable advice. VW forums are largely the same way. Keep in mind that unless someone's opinion on a forum is vetted by multiple other users, you should take it with a grain of salt. The person may or may not know what they are talking about or may not have thought about the issue from all angles. To get the most value you can out of a VW forum, I will start by outlining a couple of "don'ts".

The overwhelmingly common waste of a thread is the person who becomes a member, and their first post is a post about the car they just bought and all the grand plans they have for it. They've done almost no research, are clearly in over their heads and are asking all types of questions that could have been answered with a simple search. For example, "I just bought this Mk2 8v GTI not running. What do I need to check first to get it running? Also, what's the cheapest and easiest way to get 250 WHP out of the 8v engine that's in it?" These types of posts usually result in the person disassembling the car over the course of a few days and the thread trickling to a stop. The best-case scenario is the person at least mentions that they sold the car and asks for the thread to be deleted. Otherwise it just wastes people's time and draws the ire of senior forum trolls.

The second most common waste of a thread is the person trying to troubleshoot a problem without the proper knowledge or tools. This person also does little or no searching for information. For example, they might say, "My Mk5 misfires when I first start it in the morning. I took it to the auto parts store and they said it's missing on cylinder 1. I don't know much about cars, but I'm hoping to figure this out because it's my daily driver." The first responses are usually sarcastic answers with graphic representations of the search button and perhaps some obscenities. After that, some thoughtful, altruistic person will usually give a list of things to check, in order and report back. Invariably, the original poster ignores two-thirds of the list and says they checked things but can't describe how they checked them. From here, this typically goes one of two unfortunate ways. Either the person's car craps out completely before they can figure out the problem, or they eventually vanish and never let anyone know if the problem was fixed or what it took to fix it.

This may sound like a little bit of a rant, and it is. Mine, and a lot of people's frustrations come from people not researching and becoming familiar with a topic before they feel the need to post about it. I invite anyone who is interested to join a VW forum, but please read as much as you can and research the topic you are interested in before deciding to post. If your car is more than about five years old, whatever issue you have or question you have has probably been answered before. Sometimes many times over. I love an enthusiastic new build thread that follows a car's transformation. I love when someone finds a new solution to an old problem. I love it when members of the community come together to help someone solve a problem. I just get sick of the multitude of abandoned threads or threads asking basic questions that clog up the forums or give poor advice to someone searching for answers in the future.

The other point I'd like to make about VW forums is that you can meet some really great people, get some really great ideas and get help to challenging problems, but there are also a lot of people who are just out to prove to themselves how much they know. My request is please be respectful and helpful to others. You won't have to read very far to find people taking things way too personally or being insulting for seemingly no reason. It's just like in baseball. You can criticize the umpire's call, but if you start criticizing the umpire personally, you'll get thrown out out of the game, quick. If someone has an opinion or gives advice you don't agree with, try to politely tell them you disagree and support your position with whatever information you can. If you still can't agree, agree to disagree and move on with your life. At the end of the day, no one cares about your internet status. It's OK to be a little cynical or cheeky, but it's not OK to insult people. This will almost always end badly. As far as I can tell, the word "butthurt" had its genesis in online car forums, and you'd have a hard time finding a larger group of butthurt people in any one place at one time. Please don't be one of them.

On a more positive note, one of the best parts of online forums in my opinion are build threads. These chronicle the steps the owner took from start to finish (if there ever really is a finish with a car build). One of the most interesting, gratifying things is to read someone's build thread, start to finish. Not only does it help you realize what incredible things are possible, but that a car truly is a sum of its parts. All it takes to make a really nice car (besides money) is to keep doing work, day after day, part after part. I usually make a build thread for whatever car is my main project at the time. None of mine, personally, have been very epic, but they definitely help keep me motivated. The combination of other people's encouragement and the guilt of not having posted in a while are always enough to get me out in the garage, even if it's just to chip away at something small. Also, it's gratifying to look back on a timeline of all the hard work, time and money you invested in your car. (It doesn't hurt to link to your build thread when selling your car in the classifieds, either, but that shouldn't be your main reason.)

Instagram is a very useful app for the car community. It's really easy to set up a profile and start posting car-related photos. Also, you can follow friends, builders, shops, car shows - really anything you can think of. It's also nice to be able to search by hashtags internationally. If you're really into Mk1s, you can try #mk1monday. If you're into Mk3s, you can search for #burnallthemk3s. Instantly (hence the name), you can find hundreds, thousands or even tens of thousands of photos about a certain topic. It's nice to follow other people's builds, keep up with friends between shows or people in far-away places and follow trend-setters in the community. Frankly, it's easy to get lost scrolling and searching through Instagram. My only advice here is not to criticize others. Whether they realize it or not, everyone who participates on Instagram is looking for some kind of feedback or affirmation from other people. They are not trying to wake up in the morning and share a piece of their life looking for negative feedback. "If you can't say nuthin nice, don't say nuthin at all."

A newer trend I've seen is region or topic-specific groups on Facebook. This has been a great resource for me, both for technical advice and for buying and selling harder-to-find parts locally. In your Facebook searchbar, search for pages you might be interested in, like "[your state] VW parts" or "[your state] wheels" or "Mk4." I have bought and sold parts and cars this way and had access to information and other owners that might be hard to find anywhere else. There is even a function now where you can list things for sale, classifieds-style.

As of this writing, PayPal is the dominant way for people to pay other individuals (and many companies) for parts that are out-of-town and need to be shipped. From my experience, it's a really convenient payment solution. I only have two pieces of advice: unless the person you are buying from really is your friend or family member, don't send them money as a family or friend. Negotiate who will be responsible for the PayPal fees when you are agreeing to buy the part, but pay for it as a good or service. That's the only way you get buyer protection from PayPal. It doesn't happen a lot, but it *does happen* that a seller will take people's money for parts and not ship the parts. This has happened to people I know, more than once. It may cost you a small percentage of the purchase price, but in my opinion the peace of mind that you will get what you asked for, in the condition you expected, or your money back is totally worth it. The other piece of advice I would offer is to give some thought to using PayPal if you are on the *receiving end* of a larger sum of money. PayPal is an excellent service with lots of great features and benefits, there's no denying it. However, I have heard of buyers being unreasonable and asking for their money back or pointing out condition issues that are unreasonable and PayPal will tie up the funds for days (or weeks) or simply offer a refund when it may or may not have been fair to do so.

Pretend you sold a $3,000 car on eBay and accepted payment through PayPal. The buyer picks up the car and takes it home and then contacts PayPal and says, "You didn't disclose that xxx part needed to be replaced. I want my money back." How would you handle this, and how long will it take to get your money? Suppose that's not even possible; think of the pain and cost involved in selling your car again. PayPal is fantastic for small transactions and *paying for* large transactions, but I would do some more research before deciding to use it to *accept payment for* large transactions. There aren't many commonly-used other options for long-distance transactions at the moment, but technology moves quickly. I recommend doing a brief search. Also, there's the possibility that PayPal learns from this kind of feedback and starts handling these transactions differently.

Future of the Scene

For 60 to 70 years, the car hobby has been huge. Over the last few years though, it seems to have fallen off a little in popularity. I think one main cause is the idea that every student needs a college degree. There are fewer people looking for blue-collar work straight out of high school or trade school. Fewer young people want to work with their hands these days. It's almost impossible to participate in the car hobby if you don't want to work with your hands and/or don't have any money (like a lot of young people right now). I also argue that the myth that every kid needs to go to college puts a giant monkey on the back of a lot of kids. It's OK to work with your hands. There are excellent, fulfilling careers everywhere you look. In an age of cubicles, meetings, corporate synergy, computers and digital everything, working on a car can be cathartic. I know it is for me. If you want to read an excellent book on this topic, check out *Shop Class as Soulcraft* by Matthew Crawford.

The other main factor I see is that fewer young people are even getting a driver's license in the first place, or delaying when they do get it. According to a recent study done at the University of Michigan, "For 16- through 44-year-olds, there was a continuous decrease in the percentage of persons with a driver's license for the years examined. For example, the percentages for 20- to 24-year-olds in 1983, 2008, 2011, and 2014 were 91.8%, 82.0%, 79.7%, and 76.7%, respectively"

The bottom line is that getting a driver's license on your 16th birthday is no longer the huge milestone it used to be. Lots of high-school-aged kids don't drive at all. The car for teenagers of the '60s, '70s, '80s and '90s is being replaced by the cell phone, headphones, sneakers and video games by kids of today. There's nothing wrong with that. The big question is: where are we headed from here? Will young people eventually come around to the American car paradigm and start buying cars en masse? Will the car bug skip a generation? Is this the beginning of an even more significant and permanent trend towards the self-driving cars and Ubers of the world and away from car ownership? A lot of people have guesses and a lot of companies are betting big on what they think the outcome might be, but the truth is that no one knows for sure.

What I do know is that there are few things in life as exhilarating as throttling through a curvy mountain road with your windows down. There are few things that can top the tingle in your spine when you feel the sound of a VR6 at full throttle when the intake runners switch. My guess is that kids aren't as into cars right now because they've never ridden in a car with a manual transmission or crank windows, let alone a classic or modified car. Kids are holed up in their rooms playing video games or on their cell phone on a Friday night instead of driving around with their friends. This is not a complaint; I'm just pointing out a trend I've noticed. The problem I see is that of a childhood full of riding in the back of an

SUV or run-of -the-mill commuter car not leaving them with any kind of nostalgia when they're older and have more disposable income.

I would argue that it's a problem of kids not knowing about the hobby, as opposed to knowing about the hobby and not choosing it. Your average 17-year-old kid has never ridden in any VW older than a Mk4. It's not even on their radar to pick up an inexpensive Mk2 or Mk3 as a project. We all need to do a better job of talking about the scene and we all need to invite people to come to our shows, ride in our cars and hang out at our garages. Also, once kids find out about the hobby, the barrier for entry for most kids seems too high. It seems to require too much time and money. You have to pay for a car, insurance, gas, license, tools, etc. etc. etc. But, the thrill of driving a car that you've worked on yourself is hard to measure. The thrill of taking something apart yourself and repairing it or improving it using your own hands is hard to measure. The pride you feel when other people recognize the hard work you have put into your car is hard to measure. In the days of immediate gratification, this type of reward for hard work might seem daunting to a young kid. What's easy to understand, though, is riding shotgun in a friend's convertible and seeing all the smiles and thumbs up, smelling the smells and hearing the growl of the engine as you accelerate.

I predict the image and demand for commuter cars might continue to evolve into that of an appliance. Some people in metros will move further away from owning a commuter car at all. With mass transportation improvements, ride sharing solutions like Uber, there really isn't a need for some people to own a car. Even in the suburbs and rural areas, people won't feel the need for their car to be a flashy status symbol. Beyond commuter cars though, I think weekend cars, collector cars and modified cars will remain as strong as ever. I think people can accept basic transportation for getting to work or school but can't accept not having a weekend car to take on a date, to car shows or rip through the mountains.

If I am right, and for the VW scene to sustain it's size and maybe even grow in the future, it's everyone's responsibility to bring others into the hobby. A lot of these kids don't own a car or have never thought about it as a hobby or a lifestyle. Ask them if they'd like to tag along to the next show. Ask them if they'd like to go for a ride in your car. Share interesting Facebook or Instagram posts with them. The VW scene is contagious, but you have to be subjected to it to catch the fever.

Also, for the VW scene to thrive, the media companies, parts companies and dealers need to change the way they communicate. They need to move towards speaking to young people in the way young people choose to communicate. That means walking around shows and sending Snaps of all the cool stuff for the people who couldn't make it. That means Instagramming or Snapchatting (or whatever the next technology is) unusual cars that come into the shop. Also, it means being more accepting of the fact that new people might have different tastes. Tastes and trends change all the time. Once more young people have gotten involved in the scene, they will probably start doing new things to cars that we haven't seen or thought of yet. That's not a bad thing (unless they're irreparably damaging their car, and even then I'd still be at least a little excited about their enthusiasm). The VW scene needs a periodic new group of owners and breath of fresh air to keep it going.

The modified VW scene might be an unusual hobby. Sometimes I find it hard to explain to friends, coworkers and family why I'm out in the garage for hours on a Sunday tinkering on my car, or why I spend all year looking forward to a show or why nobody can keep up with which car I'm working on at any given moment. Some people think I'm quirky and I guess you'd say they're right.

What I have learned after so many years is that, first of all, it's OK to be different. Some people won't understand your irrational love for VWs. That's OK. Second of all, repeated, focused hard work towards a specific goal almost always pays off. It's not the people who acquire the most expensive parts. It's not the people who buy someone else's finished car. It's the people who get out there every day and do the hard work needed to achieve their goals. Whether that's working hard on your own car or working hard at your job to pay for your car, in the end, the only way to get what you want is effort and hard work.

Third, a lot of the people I value most in my life came about through my love for VWs. Relationships I already had with some people have become even more enhanced because of it. This was probably the most surprising thing to me about this scene. I knew from a pretty young age I was going to be a VW fan for life, but I thought it would make me different and I'd have to compartmentalize it. It turns out that there are cool people out there that feel the same way, and that makes for great relationships.

Fourth, it's really hard to do for a lot of people, but you have to leave ego and jealousy out of it. All you can do is make the very best car you can and be the very best friend or family member you can be. It's like golf. Everyone has a different skill level and level of commitment. Not everyone is Tiger Woods, and that's OK. All you can do is keep practicing, keep working, and be the best you can be. Every time you learn a new skill or modify a new part of your car, you're going to feel better and better about it. You may never build a Best in Show type of car, but few people do. Set a goal for yourself, whatever it may be and get out there, put in the hard work day after day, and you will succeed. You might make some friends (like I have), meet your spouse (like I did), find a career (like I did), and learn the value of hard work and commitment (like I did) along the way.

The foundation of the future of the VW scene is made up of the people. I think we should be encouraging to anyone who wants to get involved. Be generous with your time and advice. Be welcoming to people from different generations who might have different ideas or communicate in different ways. Please preserve the truly rarest cars and parts. Please don't be wasteful or destructive with cars that are difficult or impossible to replace. Please be creative and keep pushing the creative boundaries. Please don't feel like your style has to fit in or you have to be like everyone else. Please be respectful at shows so we can keep that scene alive for us and future fans to enjoy for a long time.

I'm looking forward to many more years of car building and shows and hangs with car friends. I'm looking forward to weekend afternoons in my garage, sipping a beer and tinkering with my cars. I'm looking forward to continuing to have my mind blown by creativity and new builds. One day, I hope my daughters can get involved in the scene if they decide they want to. I hope when that day comes that the scene is thriving more than ever, even with driverless cars and Uber and electric vehicles. I'm looking forward to many more years of cranking up the music, rolling down the windows, putting both hands on the wheel and throttling through a windy country road. I hope some of what I've written in this book will help you to accomplish your goals and help make the VW scene even better in some small way. We're a big, international family and life's too short to be destructive, envious, mean or jealous. Make good choices, be different, work hard every day and enjoy yourself along the way and we will all be just fine.

Made in the USA
Lexington, KY
17 May 2018